THE
SKYE
RAILWAY

The History of the Railways of the
Scottish Highlands—Vol 5

JOHN THOMAS

Revised by John Farrington

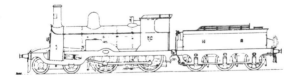

DAVID ST JOHN THOMAS PUBLISHER

THE HISTORY OF THE RAILWAYS
OF THE SCOTTISH HIGHLANDS:

Vol 1 – *The West Highland Railway*
   by John Thomas

Vol 2 – *The Highland Railway*
   by H. A. Vallance

Vol 3 – *The Great North of Scotland Railway*
   by H. A. Vallance (updated by the Great North of Scotland
   Railway Association)

Vol 4 – *The Callander & Oban Railway*
   by John Thomas (updated by John Farrington)

Vol 5 – *The Skye Railway*
   by John Thomas (updated by John Farrington)

British Library Cataloguing in Publication Data
Thomas, John *1914–1982*
The Skye railway. – New ed. – (The History of the railways
of the Scottish Highlands; 5)
1. Scotland. Highland Region. Railway
I. Title   II. Farrington, J. H. (John Hugh) *1945–*
III. Series
385.094115

ISBN 0–946537–48–8 (hbk)
      0–946537–62–3 (pbk)

First published 1977
Revised and extended edition 1990
Paperback edition first published 1991
© John Thomas 1977
© J. H. Farrington 1990

Printed in Great Britain by Redwood Press Limited,
Melksham, for David St John Thomas Publisher
PO Box 4, Nairn, Scotland IV12 4HU

Contents

NOTE TO 1990 EDITION

It was a privilege to be asked by David St John Thomas to update John Thomas' book. The author would have been intrigued to see how his 'Skye Railway' – The Kyle Line – has gone through changing fortunes since he took its story to the mid-1970s.

Oil did not turn out to be the basis for a long-term future for the line, but its future appears, in the late 1980s, to be as secure as at any time since nationalisation, for reasons explained in my extra chapter.

Obviously, it would be foolish to be complacent, especially in the present economic and political climate, but with adroit management and public support, the Skye Railway can look forward to the twenty-first century.

John Farrington

Introduction

There is nothing quite like the railway between Inverness and Kyle of Lochalsh, the Skye Railway, for most of its life very much the iron road to the Isles. At its western end it meets the sea and while serving as the railhead for Skye its days as part of the through route to the Outer Hebrides are now over. It is one of the most superb routes on British Railways, running through wild mountain scenery, in its own way quite the equal of the Swiss Alps. Yet in the cold hard world of economics it is just another meandering branch line with no hope of making a profit – it never did – and today is an anachronism. In recent years there were strong moves by authority towards closure and firm dates were announced for the service to end. It seemed that the local fight for retention was lost, but, at the eleventh hour, modern technology in the form of expanding oil exploration came to its rescue with new traffic for oil platform construction on the shores of Loch Kishorn near the western end of the line. First came a stay of execution, then the threat of closure was lifted. The Skye Railway is still there waiting to welcome those who have never sampled the delights of this magnificently scenic route, and to greet old friends returning to savour its magic once again. Though after all oil was not its saviour, tourism and better management give it a more assured future than for many years.

John Thomas's Skye Railway as many later-day enthusiasts will remember it. No 37414 with the 1130 Kyle of Lochalsh to Inverness train is photographed on 7 May 1988 by Alan Mitchell at Craig, Loch Carron.

CHAPTER 1

West of Inverness

WOOL WEEK

The year was 1864. It was Wool Week in Inverness – the week of the July sheep and wool sales – and the town was packed with important people who had gathered for what traditionally was a social as well as a business occasion.

The new Inverness & Perth Junction Railway had revolutionised Wool Week. More people than ever before had come to Inverness for the event. The trains had eliminated the long, tiresome journeys until then demanded of the participants, and for most of them Inverness was but a few hours distant. Not only did the railway benefit the lairds and the farmers, but the beasts, too, arrived by train fresh and fit instead of tired, dusty and short of weight after days, even weeks, on the rough Highland drove roads.

The railway system round Inverness in that summer of 1864 was a magnificent example of Highland self help. Railway speculators in the south had left the Highlands severely alone; they saw scant chance of squeezing dividends out of a remote region of moor, mountain and heather, starved of the coal, minerals and urban population held to be prerequisites for the profitable operation of a railway. The Highlanders waited for nearly 20 years and, when there was no sign of a railway being built from the Lowlands into the Highlands they built a railway from the Highlands into the Lowlands using native personnel and skills and mostly their own money.

Three remarkable men dominated the Highland railway scene – Sir Alexander Matheson, Joseph Mitchell and Andrew Dougall. Matheson, an eastern merchant who had

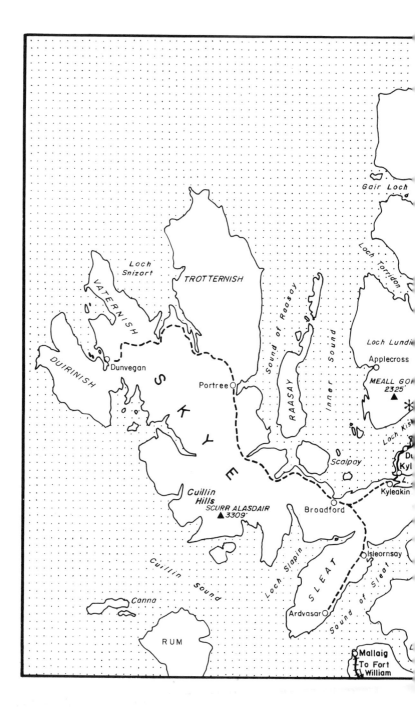

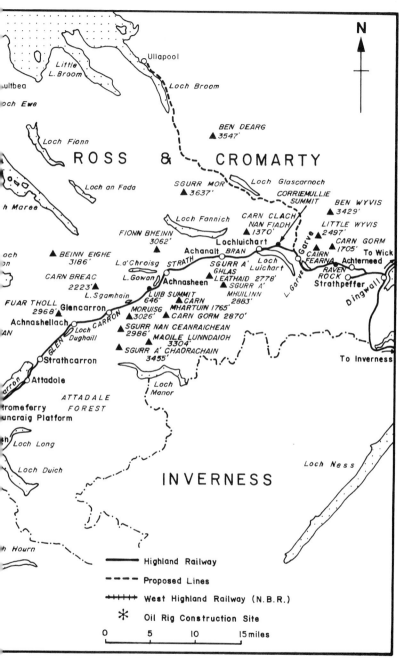

N

Ullapool
Little
L. Broom
ultbea
Loch Broom
och Ewe

BEN DEARG
▲ 3547'

Loch Fionn

R O S S   &   C R O M A R T Y

Loch an Fada
SGURR MOR
▲ 3637'
Loch Glascarnoch
CORRIEMULLIE
SUMMIT
h Maree
Loch Fannich
CARN CLACH
NAN FIADH
▲1370'
BEN WYVIS
▲ 3429'
LITTLE WYVIS
▲ 2497'
FIONN BHEINN
3062'
Lochluichart
Achanalt BRAN
CARN GORM
1705' To Wick
och
on
▲ BEINN EIGHE
3186'
L.a'Chroisg STRATH
SGURR A'
GHLAS
Loch
Luichart
CAIRN
FEARNA
Achterneed
CARN BREAC
2223'▲
L.Gowan
Achnasheen
LEATHAID 2778'
▲ SGURR A'
RAVEN
ROCK
Strathpeffer
L.Sgamhain
MHUILINN
2883'
Dingwall
FUAR THOLL
2968' Glencarron
LUIB SUMMIT
646'
▲CARN
MHARTUIN 1765'
Achnashellach
Loch
Dughaill
MORUISG
▲3026'
▲ CARN GORM 2870'
AN
SGURR NAN CEANRAICHEAN
2986'
MAOILE LUNNDAIOH
3304'
Strathcarron
▲ SGURR A' CHAORACHAIN
3455'
To Inverness

Attadole
Loch
Manor
ATTADALE
FOREST
romeferry
uncraig Platform

Loch Long
Loch Ness

Loch Duich
I N V E R N E S S

h Hourn

Highland Railway

- - - - Proposed Lines

++++++ West Highland Railway (N.B.R.)

∗ Oil Rig Construction Site

0   5   10   15 miles

Map of the Dingwall & Skye Railway and the extension to Kyle of
Lochalsh, and the major proposals for lines not built to Ullapool and on the
island of Skye.

accumulated great wealth and who owned the castles of Ardross and Duncraig, returned to devote his fortune to the development of his neglected homeland. Joseph Mitchell, civil engineer of Inverness, had learned his craft under the great Thomas Telford when he was building the Caledonian Canal. Later he became Superintendent of Highland Roads and Bridges, and now he was applying his unique talents to the development of the Highland railway system. Andrew Dougall, a young man of stern demeanour, stentorian voice and a gift for organisation, came from Perth seeking a career in the Highlands. Between them the three men financed, constructed and managed the railways built out of Inverness.

The Inverness & Nairn was the first of Mitchell's railways. It was a modest affair running for 15 miles eastwards from Inverness along the shore of the Moray Firth. It was opened on 6 November 1855 and managed by Andrew Dougall. By 18 August 1858 the railway had been extended eastwards to Keith under the name of the Inverness & Aberdeen Junction Railway to join the Great North of Scotland Railway and provide communication between Inverness and Aberdeen, and to the south via Forfar, Perth and Stirling. On 17 May 1861 the I & AJ absorbed the Inverness & Nairn. By then the Matheson-Mitchell-Dougall trio was pushing a line northwards out of Inverness. The Ross-shire Railway was opened to Dingwall on 11 June 1862 and to Invergordon on 25 March 1863.

It was in that year that the Inverness triumvirate scored its greatest triumph. On 9 September 1863 the great Inverness & Perth Junction Railway was opened throughout from Forres on the I & AJ to an end-on junction with an existing railway at Dunkeld in Perthshire. Never before had Britain seen a railway like this. It ran south for 103 miles, twice in its course crossing mountain barriers, first Dava at a summit of 1052ft then Druimuachdar Pass 1484ft above sea level. (Druimuachdar was, and remains, the highest point in Britain reached by a main line railway.) Magnificently engineered, the line swept in easy curves through the glens and over the mountain passes. And Joseph Mitchell built it all in 23 months. At last Inverness had direct rail communication with the south.

And so it came about in July 1864 trains brought people to Wool Week from north, east and south – but not from the west. The western seas were barely 70 miles across country from Inverness as the crow flies. The Isle of Skye was part of Inverness-shire, but few Skyemen or their families had seen their county town. To reach it from Skye overland involved an expedition over a primitive mountain road, through difficult country with few inhabited places. It was not surprising that the triumvirate should turn its attention to forcing the mountain barrier by taking a railway through to the west coast.

The railway trunk route north of Inverness clung to the narrow, fertile coastal plain keeping to the eastern fringe of the mountainous central regions of Ross-shire and Sutherland. There was only one lateral glen system in Ross-shire. It opened up opposite Dingwall 18¾ miles from Inverness and extended across the county to the sea lochs in the west. Two secondary glen systems branched off the main valley and struck north west towards the coast. The first, diverging at Garve, twelve miles from Dingwall, gave access to Ullapool a semi-derelict fishing port established in 1788 by the British Fisheries Society, and the second, beginning at Achnasheen 27½ miles from Dingwall, provided a route via Loch Maree to the coastal village of Gairloch.

The few hardy travellers who ventured west of the plains of Easter Ross soon found themselves in a barren, lonely land given over to sheep and deer. There were patches of soil along the valleys of streams and round the basins of mountain-girt lochs, but naked rock and heather-covered moorland dominated the landscape. Here and there stood isolated houses occupied for a few months of the year by wealthy gentlemen, usually of non-Highland origin, who desired and were willing to pay for solitude. It was not by accident that the glens were empty. In the hideous days of the Clearances during the eighteenth and early nineteenth centuries the once flourishing crofting population had had their houses burned around them and they themselves were driven like cattle to the coast and the emigrant ships to make the land safe for the deer and the sheep.

The central east-west valley and its offshoots eventually

reached the belt of rock which runs up the whole length of the
west coast from Lochalsh to Cape Wrath and penetrates inland
for 10 or 20 miles. To the geologists it was 'a belt of gneiss over-
lain in many parts by Torridonian sandstone and flanked by
Cambrian limestone and quartzites.' To the traveller it was a
spectacle of unparalleled grandeur. To the railway builder it
presented a mighty challenge. Somewhere on that beautiful
but, to the engineer, inhospitable coast, was to be created a new
port to serve the islands and a railway taken to it through the
formidable hinterland.

The shortest route from Dingwall to the west coast was by
Garve to Ullapool, a distance of 45 miles. The passage was easy
enough – for those regions – until it reached the coastal rock
belt when it took an abrupt plunge down to the shores of Loch
Broom. By Achnasheen to Gairloch was 60 miles, but stiff gradients and extensive rock cutting ruled it out for railway building. That left the main glen system.

The first positive step in the creation of the Skye railway was
taken by nine gentlemen who gathered in a room at 27 Abing-
don Street, Westminster, London, on 26 April 1864 to hear
what Joseph Mitchell and Andrew Dougall had to say about
the proposed line. The choice of venue, at first sight incongruous, was dictated by the fact that several of the people concerned had business at one or other of the Houses of
Parliament. Vice Chancellor Sir John Stuart was in the chair.
Notable Highlanders like MacLeod of MacLeod, MacLeod of St
Kilda and Sir Alexander Matheson were there. The Duke of
Sutherland, himself about to build a railway of his own in the
north, was represented by his agent Mr Loch. Mr Tennant was
in attendance at the request of Lord Hill whose lands straddled
the route of the Skye railway.

Joseph Mitchell gave details of a survey he had made of what
he considered to be the shortest practicable route from east to
west. He pointed out Dingwall on the map and traced the line
westwards through Strathpeffer and on by Garve to Loch Luichart then by Strath Bran and Glencarron to reach salt water
where Loch Carron thrust its fiord-like arm in from the sea.
The final 18 miles was along the south shore of Loch Carron to

a point on the coast opposite Kyleakin in Skye. The railway would be 67 miles long and would put Skye within 86 miles of Inverness. Referring to the country to be traversed in his memoirs Mitchell was to write:

> Although the population was sparse the district to be served was vast, the resources of the country were wholly undeveloped, particularly the fisheries which were inexhaustible and as the scenery along the line was unsurpassed in Scotland for beauty, variety and grandeur it was thought that a cheap line in this direction would be fairly remunerative.

Andrew Dougall produced a traffic estimate. On the whole of the west coast of Scotland north of the Clyde there was not a single rail-connected port. Fish caught in the rich fishing grounds of the Minches had to be taken either to the Clyde or round the north of Scotland to the east coast ports. Fish so handled was no longer fresh, and only fresh fish commanded good prices in the urban markets. The most lucrative market of all was London, but only fish of prime quality was acceptable at Billingsgate market. The new railway would put the western fishing grounds within easy reach of London for the first time. Fish traffic would be a staple revenue earner for the railway. Skye sheep carried in crowded vessels to winter quarters in eastern Scotland would travel quickly by train to their destinations and return the same way. The people of the islands and west coast would at last have a speedy and easy route not only to Inverness but to all parts of Britain, and tourists, no longer faced with the long sea voyage from Glasgow, would be tempted to seek out the magic of the islands. Above all the railway would unlock the beautiful but seldom-seen country between Dingwall and the west coast. True enough there was hardly a village on the route worthy of the name – except Strathpeffer which had a secluded situation and mineral waters of repute. The railway might well be the catalyst that would turn Strathpeffer into a prosperous spa resort. Dougall was confident that the railway would pay a dividend of $4\frac{1}{2}$ per cent.

The gentlemen were sufficiently impressed to agree to meet again in the same place in two days' time. Dougall was told to prepare a prospectus. There was a discussion on what the railway would be called and it was decided to name it the Skye Railway.

At the meeting on 28 April the participants constituted themselves into a provisional committee. Mitchell was appointed engineer and Dougall secretary, both being warned that 'they shall look to the undertaking itself for their remuneration and not to the committee as individuals.' Some further discussion took place on the name of the railway and it was resolved that it be changed to the Dingwall & Skye Railway. All that remained now was to present the scheme to the public, solicit subscriptions and obtain an Act of Parliament. It was agreed that no better time and place could be chosen for the initial promotion than Wool Week in Inverness.

After lunch on Friday 15 July – the last day of Wool Week – many of the local and visiting notables could be seen drifting in the direction of the Caledonian Hotel. A reporter from the *Northern Chronicle* who edged his way into the reception room found the place so congested that he had difficulty in picking out and identifying the celebrities present. For once his cliche 'a numerous and influential gathering' had substance. It was plain to him that many would be more at home in a castle than a cottage. He jotted down the names of a clutch of clan chiefs, two baronets and three Members of Parliament. Bankers, ministers and factors of estates joined the throng. The reporter recognised Cameron of Lochiel, Sir Kenneth Mackenzie, Sir Alexander Gordon-Cumming of Altyre, Major Fraser-Tytler of Aldourie, General Macdonald and many others. Matheson, Mitchell and Dougall circulated among the assembly. At least the new railway was to be launched in a rarefied social atmosphere.

MacLeod of MacLeod called the meeting to order. There could not have been a more appropriate chairman. The Macleod's ancestral home, Dunvegan Castle in Skye, was barely 80 miles away, but the easiest route from Dunvegan to Inverness was by steamer to Glasgow and then back by rail over the Grampians to Inverness, a distance of nearly 500 miles occupying at least two days. The chairman told his audience, 'This town is undoubtedly the county town, but at present I call Glasgow my county town because I go there for everything I want by means of the steamers.'

The MacLeod enumerated the benefits the railway would bring:

> It is very well known that our seas teem with fish at the present moment and that our lochs are full of herrings, but the difficulty is to procure barrels and salt and markets. We all know that the way in which sheep are conveyed by means of steamers is one very much to be regretted but which many have been compelled to adopt. By such means they are hashed and knocked about as many present will testify in a manner that cannot fail to injure them severely.

The chairman's remarks struck a responsive chord in at least one member of his audience who affirmed:

> My sheep are generally a month in travelling to Falkirk and even then a great deal of their fat is taken off them whereas if we had a line of railway a day or two would be the extent of the time consumed.

One jaundiced listener spoke of the railway's catchment area as 'sterile country having on its seaboard a population little removed from the verge of pauperism.' But another speaker was quick to point out that the railway enriched the land wherever it went and would surely enrich the impoverished west. He said, 'With regard to the condition of the labouring classes of the west coast my belief is that from the time of the opening of the railway we will hear no more word of emigration.'

The MacLeod spoke of generous offers of help. The Duke of Sutherland had intimated that he would take £5,000 worth of stock and 12 landowners had earmarked shares to the value of £40,000 between them. Three landowners on the route of the railway expressed their intention to accept stock in payment for land required for the line, Matheson to the extent of 24 miles, Lord Hill 14 miles and the Duke of Sutherland three miles; 41 miles of the total 67 miles were thus accounted for. The MacLeod made it seem very easy, but he cautioned:

> Can we make it? In the first place I must tell you it requires the co-operation of every individual interested in the country through which the line must pass. What I wish to impress earnestly upon you is this, that the proposed railway cannot be made unless all come forward strenuously to aid us. You cannot get the public to subscribe towards the construction of a railway unless they are interested in it and come forward and show their interest in it by subscribing largely.

Sir Kenneth MacKenzie agreed, but claimed that there was little hope of getting money from the south. Such was the enthusiasm of the meeting that southern support seemed unnecessary. 'I will take 50 shares,' announced Stuart of Ellanreoch. 'An example well worthy of imitation,' commented The MacLeod, and there was a rumble of approval round the room.

FIGHTING FEUDALISM

On 10 October 1865, 15 months after the euphoric Wool Week meeting the more sombre first ordinary meeting of the shareholders of the Dingwall & Skye Railway heard the chairman Alexander Matheson report:

> In consequence of unforeseen difficulties which have arisen in arranging with certain landowners on the line no progress had been made with the works and the directors think it right to state that no steps will be taken until these difficulties are removed.

A year passed before the directors again faced the shareholders. On 30 October 1866 the chairman told them:

> The directors have to report that in consequence of the state of the money market during the last 12 months the works have not been commenced and they regret to say that the difficulty in arranging with certain landowners on the line alluded to in the last report still exists.

In two years the directors had spent £14,126 17s 10d on legal and other preliminaries and there was not an inch of railway to show for it. What had gone wrong?

At the first business meeting of the company on 6 October 1864 Andrew Dougall tabled a list of subscribers. Shares at £10 each had been subscribed to the value of £101,160, exclusive of the value of stock given in exchange for land. By subscribing the subscriber agreed to accept a specific number of shares which he would pay for by instalments or 'calls' when requested to do so by the company. No money changed hands in the first instance. It cost nothing to become a subscriber. What Dougall held was a parcel of paper promises.

The company's money troubles began when the subscription list, after the first flush of enthusiasm, refused to grow. Not only were new subscribers slow in coming forward, but some of the existing subscribers showed reluctance to being parted from their money. Some had second thoughts about the railway and wanted to be relieved of their obligations. The company took a firm line with defaulters. They were told that their promise to take up shares was legally binding and that the company would take them to court to enforce payment. When in December 1864 Dougall reported that Dochfour 'demurs accepting the 500 shares alloted to him', the board resolved 'to instruct Messrs Martin and Leslie to raise an action in the Court of Queen's Bench against Dochfour for the full amount of £5000'. The black list contained distinguished names, among them Lord Listowel, Sir James Matheson and The MacLeod himself who was deputy chairman of the company. Dougall wrote to all of them without fear or favour reminding them of the dire consequences of their failure to meet their calls and stating that all shareholders still in arrears on 15 January would be prosecuted for payment of the amount due plus interest.

The money problem, although serious was not the most immediate of the Skye line's worries. The sad fact was that there were those who did not want a railway in Wester Ross. People who had paid for solitude were determined to preserve it at all costs, and they fought the railway tooth and nail. The spirit of the Clearances lingered on. Even landowners who were shareholders would permit the railway to pass only on a path dictated by them irrespective of what the engineer said. If they did not get their own way they threatened to oppose the forthcoming Bill in Parliament.

Davidson of Tulloch was one shareholder who turned sour over the chosen route of the railway. The configuration of the ground at the eastern end meant that the railway had to sweep away from Dingwall in a wide north to west curve before entering the valley of the Peffery, and Mitchell had chosen the obvious route along the north side of the Dingwall canal. Tulloch wanted the line to go along the south side of the canal and he let it be known that if the company did not meet his wishes he

would oppose the Bill. The company arranged a meeting
chaired by the Provost of Dingwall at which each side stated its
case. But there was no placating Tulloch. The directors well
knew that to move the railway from north to south of the canal
would be to jump from the frying pan into the fire. As well as
tightening an already sharp curve the shift would have meant
that the railway was encroaching on the sacrosanct property of
the Free Church. In the end Tulloch was persuaded to submit
the dispute to the President of the Institute of Civil Engineers
for arbitration 'with power to him to determine which of the
two is to be preferred having regard to the safe and convenient
working of the railway and of the Ross-shire Extention Railway.' The President decided in favour of the Dingwall & Skye.
Tulloch stubbornly refused to accept his judgement and went
on with his plans to fight the Bill. The MacLeod tried to
appease him by offering to pay his accumulated legal fees of
£300, but the offer was spurned.

Lord Hill next entered the field as an opponent of the Bill.
The directors bought him off, but not until they had changed
the route so that the line passed behind his house and not in
front as planned, agreed to divert the turnpike road at the front
of the house and had guaranteed his lordship a private platform. Lady Ashburton, too, made threatening noises. Her price
for allowing the railway to pass through her estate in the neigh-
bourhood of Loch Luichart was £4000 'land and residential
damage' plus the almost obligatory private station.

The sorest thorn in the Skye line's flesh was Sir William
MacKenzie of Coul. He announced that 'unless certain propositions as to the course of the line and the nature of the works
be conceded' he would oppose the Bill. One of his propositions
was that the railway must be carried in tunnel through a part of
his estate where a tunnel was neither practicable nor necessary,
and·that the railway would be elaborately camouflaged to sug-
gest to the observer that it did not exist. MacKenzie's threat
had serious implications. If the company refused to accept his
demands the railway would be refused access to Strathpeffer,
the only place on the route with a worthwhile population.
Nevertheless, the board resolved to reject all MacKenzie's

propositions and dug themselves in to do battle at Westminster.

Ignoring his company's drastic financial position and the seemingly implacable hostility of the feudal mandarins Dougall pressed on with the preparation of the Bill. He found a bank willing to lend money for the obligatory Parliamentary deposit and the Bill was presented. Its passage through Parliament was unexpectedly easy. Westminster was having a fit of conscience about the plight of the Western Highlands and the government of the day sensed that if it dealt harshly with the first railway scheme aimed at serving the district it might suffer at the ballot box. The opposition although determined was over-ridden and the Dingwall & Skye Railway Act was passed on 5 July 1865. It authorised the company to build 63 miles of railway from Dingwall to Kyle of Lochalsh and to create a port out of nothing at the terminus 'and on the soil or bed of the sea adjacent thereto.' The piers were to occupy 300yd of the shoreline and extend for 300yd into the sea. The company was empowered to acquire or lease the existing ferry between Kyle of Lochalsh and Kyleakin in Skye and to build a hotel at Kyle. It was an ambitious package for a concern that did not know where its next penny was coming from.

A clause in the Act headed 'For the Protection of the Estate of Coul' revealed how far the company had gone to placate Mac-Kenzie. 'It is expedient that the railway should be carried through the same with as little detriment as possible.' This meant that, among other things, over a length of 12 miles 7 furlongs no spoil was to be deposited without the consent of Sir William. At a point starting 6 miles and 6 furlongs west of Dingwall the railway was to be carried for 510yd, 'in a tunnel or be covered with arching to the satisfaction and sight of an engineer to be appointed by the said Sir William MacKenzie. Such arching shall be at the expense of the company, be covered with soil as nearly as may be on the natural slope of the ground and be sown with and maintained in grass and the slopes of all cuttings and embankments on the said estate of Coul shall, at the expense of the company, be dressed and finished and afterwards maintained in a neat and efficient manner. The said Sir William MacKenzie his heirs and successors shall be entitled to the free occupation in all time coming to the surface over the said tunnel or arching and make such use thereof as he or they shall think fit.' The Act allowed the company to spend £4350 on the landscaping of the railway in the estate of Coul.

In the history of any normal railway the granting of the Act is a key date, an occasion for pride and rejoicing. The promotional pains are behind them and the directors are free to devote their whole energies to the construction of the line. The Dingwall & Skye was not a normal railway. To the hostile factions the Act was little more than a scrap of paper and the harassment of the directors continued. On the very day Dougall laid the Act on the boardroom table – 2 August 1865 – he reported that he had written to Tulloch, Sir William MacKenzie of Coul, the agents of the Kilcoy Trustees and the factor for the Strathcarron properties 'to inquire on what terms they will allow the line to pass through their respective properties, but that no replies had yet been received.'

An enterprising builder inserted advertisements in the local papers announcing that ground for houses would presently be let at Strathpeffer and he made much of the fact that the ground would be adjacent to the station. Dougall saw fit to inform the advertiser that he was counting his chickens before they were hatched. By this time the obstacles in the first six miles of the line seemed so formidable that the directors were almost convinced that the railway would never get away from Dingwall. On 30 January 1866 Dougall took the drastic step of instructing the engineer to survey *without delay* a new line which would leave the Ross-shire Railway at Conon Bridge south of Dingwall and strike through Brahan and Contin to a point west of the Falls of Rogie where it would join the Parliamentary line. The survey was delivered on 10 February and at a board meeting four days later it was decided to approach the Seaforth Trustees with a view to acquiring land for the proposed deviation.

The Brahan project proved to be a damp squib. A summer a winter and another summer passed with nothing accomplished. The subscription list remained stagnant – an apparently moribund railway scheme had no attraction for investors – and bank loans were unpaid. The directors lost heart. No board meetings at all were held between 14 February and 20 September 1867. At last Lord Middleton and three exasperated shareholders met at Jeantown and urged the board to salvage what it could of the Parliamentary line by deviating from the disputed places and terminating the line at the first deep water it met instead of taking it out to the coast. Attadale, two miles from the end of Loch Carron, seemed a likely point for a port. Following such a plan the directors could dispense with the construction of at least 12 of the most difficult miles of the railway and reduce the total cost of the undertaking to £220,000. The directors adopted the suggestion and appealed for £40,000 in new subscriptions with which to make a fresh start. They got more than half of what they asked.

At this point Dougall took stock of the company's finances and presented his findings to the board:

Original subscription list £103,000 of which . . . probably only £91,000 can be relied on	£91,000
New list laid before meeting	£26,160
Value of land which it is expected will be taken in shares, 30 miles at £200 per mile	£6000
Contributions from other railways (Assumed)	£30,000

By this reckoning the company was only £66,840 short of its target. But the estimate was too fraught with 'ifs' for comfort.

Immediate drastic economies were called for. Up to that time the company had incurred fees of about £5000 – which had not been paid – for the services of Joseph Mitchell. The directors decided that Mitchell was a luxury they could not afford and that a less prestigious engineer employed on a full time basis at a modest fee would meet their requirements. Mitchell and the Dingwall & Skye parted company. Joseph Mitchell was one of the most popular and highly respected men in the Highlands and his name alone on the prospectus had won support for the railway. Now the pilot was being dropped. It was regrettable that his going was marred by acrimony over the settling of the company's financial debt to him. In the end he got a promissory note for £3500 payable in 12 months and 50 shares. His successor was Murdoch Paterson who had been a partner in the Mitchell family firm of Joseph Mitchell & Company. His salary was £500 a year.

At the third annual general meeting on 30 October 1867 the long-suffering shareholders at last were given a glimmer of hope. They were informed:

> The directors have to state that during the past summer they had the whole route of the line carefully examined and partially resurveyed with a view to reducing the expense and they are glad to say the result has been satisfactory. By effecting alterations and deviations at several parts of the line there will not be a great saving in the cost but the route will be unobjectionable to those landowners who felt themselves compelled to oppose the original scheme.

Details of the modified route were set out in the Dingwall & Skye Railway (Deviation) Act of 1868. The first deviation extended from a point 2 furlongs west of Dingwall to a point 15 miles and 1 furlong west of Dingwall. Instead of going down the valley to the Peffery to Strathpeffer the railway now swung sharply across the valley at Fodderty and began a steep ascent of the hillside on the north side of the valley. Five miles further on it reached a summit of 458ft at Raven's Rock after which it dropped to a point near the east end of Loch Garve where it took up its original formation. MacKenzie had succeeded in hanging a grim millstone round the company's neck. Not only had he barred the railway from Strathpeffer and denied it an easy passage to the west but he had saddled it for life with a quite unnecessary deviation that was to prove difficult and expensive to operate.

The second diversion, which was made to overcome objections at the western end of the line extended for a distance of 3 miles 6 furlongs from 39 miles 2 furlongs to a point 43 miles west of Dingwall. The Act which was passed on 29 May 1868 also sanctioned the provision of a pier and hotel at Attadale on the lines of those sanctioned for Kyle of Lochalsh and now abandoned.

BUILDING THE LINE

The original Act of 1865 had specified five years for the completion of the railway. With almost three of those years gone the Dingwall & Skye board was at last in a position to proceed with the building of the railway. Tenders were invited from contractors and suppliers of materials. It was made clear that only contractors who were prepared to take up at least £2500 worth of Dingwall & Skye stock would be considered.

The construction of the line was let in two contracts, the first from Dingwall to Achanant ($21\frac{1}{2}$ miles) to J & A Granger of Perth for £63,583 16s 3d and the second from Achanant to Attadale ($27\frac{1}{2}$ miles) to A & K Macdonald of Glasgow at £62,798. Both contractors resisted the company's attempt to foist £2500 worth of stock on them. Granger took £1500 and Macdonald £2000. Two unsuccessful tenderers who had bought shares in the hope of influencing the decision of the board wanted the Dingwall & Skye to take them back. The company refused. The contract for the pier at Attadale went to Donald McGregor & Company of Dingwall for £4840 14s 4d Alexander Ross, chartered architect of Inverness designed refreshment and waiting rooms for Attadale station and a grand hotel that would stand on a terrace 20ft above the railway, and was authorised to take tenders for these works. The first sod of the Dingwall contract was cut on 2 September 1868 and the Lochcarron contract was begun a month later.

On 8 August 1868 the Dingwall & Skye had acquired a new director in the person of John Fowler of Braemore. Fowler's family seat was at Wadsley Hall, Yorkshire. A civil engineer by profession he had served with distinction with the army in Egypt and the Sudan and on his retirement had purchased a 57,300 acre estate in the Loch Broom area in remote country about 30 miles north west of the railway. He was not an easy man to get on with. As a shareholder he had interfered in the affairs of the company; he tended to consider himself an *ex officio* consulting engineer. He had put forward his own ideas for solving the Dingwall curve dispute only to have them rejected by the board, and he crossed swords with Mitchell more than once. In 1865 he whispered in the ear of the Duke of Sutherland, for whom Mitchell had surveyed the Sutherland Railway, that Mitchell was an expensive engineer and that in particular he was extravagant with his bridges. The Duke repeated the story in the board room of the Highland Railway (which was formed on 28 June 1865 by the amalgamation of the Inverness & Perth Junction and the Inverness & Aberdeen Junction) and the board upbraided Mitchell. He gently pointed out that he built his bridges to satisfy acceptable safety standards. Fowler wanted the Dingwall & Skye built to a gauge of 3ft 6in. Mitchell rejected the suggestion on the grounds that a narrow gauge line would not be able to cope with the heavy cattle and sheep traffic and that trans-shipment facilities would be required at Dingwall. Mitchell calculated that a reduction in gauge would achieve a saving of only £50,000.

Fowler clashed with Mitchell over the Raven Rock diversion. He was all for capitulating to MacKenzie whereas Mitchell considered the original route worth fighting for. The diversion passed through empty country; the original route served Strathpeffer, the village of Contin and had a superb scenic attraction in the Falls of Rogie. Mitchell saw Strathpeffer as the Harrogate of the North. He believed that the existing coach traffic of from £3000 to £4000 a year would be boosted to £8000 by the railway. Writing later about the diversion he commented, 'Mr Fowler, being a director, was consulted and in his ignorance of the country approved of this alteration.'

Fowler, soon after his appointment to the board, went down to Loch Carron to look at Attadale. He disapproved of the plans for the hotel and pier and suggested alterations, which the board refused to accept. Fowler's next move was to condemn Attadale outright as a railhead. He wanted the railway to go further down Loch Carron. The board was thrown into confusion and once more the fate of the Skye line was in the melting pot. Fowler went off to winter in the Mediterranean and left the directors with their problems. At a meeting on 4 January 1869 the chairman urged that nothing be done about fixing the site of the western terminal until the beginning of March 'by which

time it is expected that Mr Fowler will have returned from
abroad.' At the March meeting it was decided to take the railway a further $4\frac{1}{2}$ miles down Loch Carron to Strome Ferry the
extra mileage to be considered as an extension of Macdonald's
contract. The contractor agreed to build the extension for
£5232 4s 10d and McGregor was instructed to erect the pier
planned for Attadale at Strome instead.

To raise money for day-to-day expenses the board made a
call of £2 per share. The response was poor. The company was
short by £29,632 of the amount needed to complete the line only
to Attadale, and the directors found that they had underesti-
mated the cost of the extension by £2000. Nevertheless Murdoch Paterson was warned that he must not exceed the original
estimate. 'Savings to that extent must be effected and the board
rely on you not exceeding £5300,' he was told. Gone were the
plans for an imposing station and hotel. A short unpaved platform and a functional timber pier at Strome were all the company could afford. Paterson was ordered to buy steel rails for
the points and crossings only and use iron rails elsewhere. Signals were to be 'of the simplest character.'

The never-ending scrounge for money went on. Several
banks were approached for a £30,000 loan, but without success.
When the National Bank offered a loan only in exchange for the
personal cheques of the directors the board resolved 'to close
the company's account with the National Bank.' A £30,000
loan was negotiated with the Commercial Bank but only after
the Dingwall & Skye had deposited £105,000 worth of stock
with the bank.

A major cause of the company's continuing financial malaise
was the failure to take up shares by some of the original subscribers of 1864. The board decided to have another attempt to
obtain payment of debts now outstanding for nearly five years.

The MacLeod, who was still a director of the Dingwall &
Skye was deemed to be in debt to his own company to the extent
of £7000. He had offered to pay £2000 but the offer had been
refused and the company had instituted an action against him
in the Court of Queen's Bench for the full amount of his original
subscription. The MacLeod found himself in this invidious

situation partly because of a misunderstanding. When the formation of the Dingwall & Skye was under discussion in 1864 the Land Improvements Bill was before Parliament and The MacLeod thought that under this Bill he would be entitled to reclaim any money he devoted to the provision of railways in the Highlands from the Government. He explained his predicament to the Dingwall & Skye chairman in a letter written on 24 April 1869.

My Dear Matheson,
   Having been given to understand that the proposal made by Mr Brand on my behalf to take an additional 100 shares in the Dingwall & Skye Railway was not entertained by the board, I write to you as chairman to try whether it may not be possible to get this disagreeable matter settled and I make the attempt assuming that the other members of the board, all personal friends of my own, will be as willing to avoid litigation as I am, and to close the affair in an amicable manner if possible. Of course, you remember at the first meeting of the promoters of the line the proposal that I should be a subscriber to the extent of a year's rental was entirely contingent on the same being made chargeable on my entailed estate under a Bill at that time before Parliament. The Act was passed and I subsequently made inquiries which satisfied me that it could not apply to my case for reasons which I need not enter into here. In October 1864 I wrote to you suggesting that instead of the original proposal I might take 300 shares as a personal subscription, but I heard no more on the subject and indeed on making inquiry I found I should not have been able to take so many. However, I am not even aware that the proposal was ever mentioned to the board. At all events I regard it as no longer in evidence as a proposal and when subsequently calls were made I applied for and received a call paper for 100 shares on which the deposit was duly paid. This transaction brings us to the last proposal to increase my subscription by an additional 100 shares and that offer was made (I tell you quite frankly) because it was the very largest sum I found I could borrow on my own personal security. This offer having been rejected I now propose in order if possible to come to terms, to accept an allotment of a second 100 shares making 200 shares now and paying the calls as they become due and further to come under an engagement to take 100 more, half on the 1st of December 1872, and the other half on 1st December 1873.

Yours very truly,
MacLeod of MacLeod

The simple truth was that The MacLeod, like many of his Highland compatriots, had no money to spare. The board accepted his proposition.

The winter of 1868–9 was exceptionally fine. There were only ten days when work was impossible and exceptional progress was made. On 29 October 1869 the shareholders were informed:

> The directors are glad to be able to state that the works of the whole line from Dingwall to Strome Ferry, including the pier there have made satisfactory progress during the last year. The foundations for all the important bridges have been secured and the earthworks are in a very advanced state. The directors therefore entertain no doubt that the line will be opened for public traffic about the 1st July next. From additional information received during the last few months and inquiries made on the spot by some of the directors respecting the probable traffic they feel confident that previous estimates will be amply borne out by results.

To some shareholders the report must have sounded too good to be true. It was. The chairman's eulogy was greatly at variance with certain observations made by the board to Murdoch Paterson:

> The directors regret to observe from the report of the engineer that the works of Messrs Macdonald between Achanalt and the crossing of the Carron above Craig are not making the satisfactory progress which is indispensible to ensure the timeous opening of the line, and while they are persuaded that the contractor must be sincerely desirous that the expectations of the shareholders and the public as to the time of opening shall not be disappointed the board desire to convey to Messrs Macdonald that in their opinion more strenuous efforts on their part are required and they hope that the intimation of this opinion will have the effect of at once stimulating the efforts of the contractors who are of course responsible that the contract shall be duly implemented. And the meeting instructed the engineer to report to the next meeting of the board what shall have to be done by Messrs Macdonald to carry out these views.

Geography was against Macdonald. Granger on the eastern contract was able to bring in his materials over the railway as it progressed. Macdonald had to bring everything in by sea. He got his men on site in October 1868 only to find that the timber for their huts had not arrived because the vessels carrying it were held up by adverse winds. Sailing ships bound from County Durham to Loch Carron with rails and other heavy plant were delayed by up to seven weeks. Gilkes, Wilson, Pease & Company of Middlesbrough, not realising quite where Loch Carron was, quoted an unrealistic carriage-paid price for chairs. 'We were misinformed on the subject of inaccessibleness of the district for vessels,' they complained in a letter to the D & S board, and claimed an extra 8s per ton on the consignment. A board offer of 4s was refused whereupon the contract was cancelled and a new one entered into with Head, Wrightson & Company of Stockton on Tees. The delay in the delivery of supplies meant that Macdonald and his men had to cool their heels from October to February before making a start. At least the board was granted a breathing space to deal with the recalcitrant Shaw of Glencarron who, when Macdonald's men tried to enter his property 'declined to enter into any arrangement for the land or to give access for the purpose of the company's works.'

In fairness to Macdonald he had done well enough where he had been able to gain access and move in plant. It was in the inaccessible 'interior' section of the contract that the trouble lay. The difficult section by the shore of Loch Carron between Attadale and Strome was cut, ballasted and ready for the rails by the early spring of 1870. Even Murdoch Paterson was overawed by what had been accomplished at Attadale. Explaining the works to the directors he said:

> The extension runs close to the shore for nearly its whole length and on the first mile and a half from Attadale the high precipices of rock and loose rocks and boulders on the slopes on the one side and the sea – in many parts very deep close inshore – on the other make the works necessary for a line of railway look very formidable. These difficulties I am glad to say have been satisfactorily overcome. All the loose rocks and boulders on the upper slopes have been removed and the embankments made secure against the sea.

Poor Paterson; little did he know that loose boulders at Attadale would still be a problem a century later.

With the line within sight of completion the board gave thought to the method by which the railway would be worked. It was accepted that the D & S would not own its engines and rolling stock, but would ask an established company to work the line if suitable terms could be arranged. John Fowler produced a copy of an agreement between the Midland Great Northern Railway and the Great North & Western Railway of Ireland which he thought might be made the basis of a working agreement between the Highland Railway and the Dingwall &

Skye Railway. The suggested agreement provided for the Highland Railway working and maintaining the Dingwall & Skye for 10 years from the date of opening. Two trains with crews were to be provided daily at a charge of 2s per mile, the charge for additional trains being 1s 10d per mile. In addition the Skye company had to pay rental of £200 a year for the use of Dingwall station.

The Highland board and some shareholders had mixed feelings about accepting responsibility for the new railway. The directors of the Dingwall & Skye saw their railway as a valuable feeder and considered that they should get a rebate 'on all traffic thrown on to the Highland by the opening of the Skye line.' Objectors to the agreement in the Highland camp took the view that revenue from the through traffic would not cover operating costs. Highland Railway supporters of the agreement emphasised that the Dingwall & Skye was a bridge line that would bring new traffic from the islands to Dingwall from where it would pass over 162 miles of Highland metals to Perth. There was no question of the company having to build new engines and rolling stock. Engines at present doing nothing could be usefully employed on the Skye line.

The opposition was strong enough to force a postponement of the decision for three months while an inquiry was conducted into the working of a similar agreement made between the Highland and the Sutherland Railway. In the end an agreement was reached and a committee consisting of three directors each from the Highland and Skye companies was elected to work out the practical details.

The Dingwall & Skye had hoped to make an arrangement with David Hutcheson, the Western Isles steamboat operator, to provide connecting services between Portree in Skye and Stornoway. Hutcheson's boats passed Kyle of Lochalsh on their regular sailings and had the railway reached its original terminal it is likely that the boats would have called in at the railway pier. But Strome Ferry was a different proposition. To come up Loch Carron to Strome Ferry and return to its original course meant a detour of 28 miles for a Hutcheson boat. The steamboat operator refused to handle the railway traffic. That was a severe blow to the Dingwall & Skye directors who had no intention of operating boats of their own and who, in any case, had no experience of steamboat management. At the last minute they were forced to buy two secondhand ships and arrange a pattern of services for them.

The Skye line directors had set their hearts on a 1 July opening. The summer traffic to the north would be approaching full flow by then and they were determined to be in a position to benefit from it. On 30 May the directors gave the Board of Trade one month's notice of the opening and ordered Macdonald to engage as many men as were required to meet the 1 July opening. But on the same day Murdoch Paterson reported that the line would not be ready for the Board of Trade inspection until 15 July at the earliest. The appointment with the Board of Trade was cancelled and a new opening date announced – 10 August. The highlight of the opening day festivities was to be a banquet staged in the station at Strome Ferry on the arrival of the ceremonial train from Dingwall. Invitations were sent to influential people throughout the Highlands with covering letters explaining that they only had to show their invitation card to the booking clerk at their local station to obtain a free ticket to Strome.

Captain Tyler from the Board of Trade carried out his inspection on 9 August. He failed the line and forbade its opening because of faulty fencing at various places. The board sent letters to both Granger and Macdonald severely censuring them and warning them that they would be held liable for damages. The meeting then adjourned 'until such a day as a telegram is received from Mr Paterson saying the fencing is in order.' Guests who turned up on 10 August were taken for a ride on the railway free of charge.

The official opening took place on 19 August. An extract from a private letter gives a piquant glimpse of what happened at Strome Ferry that day:

> There was a dinner served in the station. A heavy piece of sackcloth was draped across one end to keep out the wind. There was whisky, claret and port served and there were pipers from Dingwall. As the feast and toasts progressed everyone forgot who was who and when the train

The Highland Railway Company.

BANQUET AT STROME FERRY,

On WEDNESDAY, 10th AUGUST.

Audit Office,

INVERNESS, 5th August 1870.

Please issue blank card tickets to STROME FERRY, to parties presenting their BANQUETTING TICKETS, and enter the number in your Daily Return. You will debit yourself with the amount in your Monthly Return for August, at 7s 6d first class, and 4s 6d third class, and the Accountant will credit you with the same as cash remitted.

Yours truly,

C. S. M'HARDY.

left on its return to Dingwall and Inverness there were few sober. The pipers managed to get well oiled and started to play again once the refreshments were finished. They could neither blow, stand up nor all play the same tune, but none of the guests seemed to notice this. MacBrayne's steamer waited for an hour to collect the captain and he certainly could not go on the bridge. Of course that is not an unknown quality of MacBrayne's staff. Time stands still for MacBrayne if there is a dram about.

Steam at Strome

On Saturday 20 August the Scottish newspapers announced the 'New and Expeditious Route' to the Western Isles. MAGNIFICENT SCENERY trumpeted the advertisements. The Dingwall & Skye promised to take passengers from Edinburgh and Glasgow to Portree in the unprecedented time of 15 hours and to Stornoway in 24 hours. The first timetable showed two trains a day (except Sundays) between Dingwall and Strome Ferry in each direction, all taking three hours for the 53-mile journey, with a local run in the evening from Dingwall to Strathpeffer and back in connection with the express train from the south. The company's steamer *Oscar* gave a daily sailing from Strome Ferry to Portree while *Jura* sailed to Stornoway on Tuesday, Thursday and Saturday returning to Strome on Monday, Wednesday and Friday.

Miles		**Down Trains**			**Up Trains**		
0	Dingwall	10.15am	4.15pm	7.55pm	11.15am	6.15pm	8.43pm
4½	Strathpeffer	10.26am	4.28pm	8.08pm	11.03am	6.02pm	8.30pm
11¾	Garve	10.45am	4.49pm		10.45am	5.40pm	
21½	Achanant	11.21am	5.15pm		10.09am	5.08pm	
27½	Achnasheen	11.45am	5.40pm		9.45am	4.45pm	
43¾	Strathcarron	12.45pm	6.44pm		8.45am	3.45pm	
53	Strome Ferry	1.15pm	7.15pm		8.15am	3.15pm	
	Portree		11.15pm		4.15am		
	Stornoway	10.45am				5.45am	

Inverness was busy in that autumn of 1870. The Franco-Prussian War had closed many of the fashionable European resorts, and more tourists than usual had come to the Highlands. The more adventurous of them took the morning train to Dingwall on the Saturday and boarded the waiting Dingwall & Skye train for a trip through territory which a week before had been all but inaccessible to the seldom-seen west coast.

The 10.15 rounded the Dingwall curve and steamed into the valley of the Peffery. At Fodderty the embankment built to take the line across to the hills on the north side blocked the valley like the earthworks of a dam. The far-from-new locomotive that the Highland Railway had seen fit to deploy on the Skye line swung across the embankment and began its climb into the hills.

The first station carried the name Strathpeffer, although the village itself was down in the valley a mile or more away. Achterneed would have been a more honest name for the station for that was the name of the adjacent crofting community. The original holdings had been given to veterans of the Highland Corps who had been recruited from the locality to fight in the American War of Independence. The Duchess of Sutherland who owned the ground round Strathpeffer station, and whose attitude to the railway was in marked contrast to that of the gentleman who had forced the line up on to its hillside perch, had provided a turning circle for coaches outside the station and converted the track linking it with the village into a road 20ft wide, with a path for pedestrians on one side. But it was a hard slog up to the station for foot passengers and coaches alike. It was much easier to go to Strathpeffer by the direct coach that plied three times a day from the centre of the village to Dingwall.

With Strathpeffer left behind the train laboured on up the hillside on a gradient of 1 in 50. Soon the hard steep face of Raven Rock was throwing back echoes of the engine's exhaust. At the summit, 458ft above sea level and $6\frac{1}{2}$ miles from Dingwall, the line veered to the north, entered a heavy rock cutting made for its reception, swung to the west again and began its penetration of the little-known interior of Ross-shire. Gone was the fertile green strath of the Peffery. Great mountains gathered round the railway. Presently the train was skirting Loch Garve. A halt was made at Garve village where the road to Ullapool struck away to the north west.

The next station, Achanalt, was nearly 10 miles away. The engine's exhaust crackled again as it lifted the train out of the hollow in which Garve lay and tackled the climb up the wide bare glen to the next summit at Corriemuillie 492ft above sea level. Once over the top it drifted down through the woods to Loch Luichart, rounded the end of the loch and swung into Strath Bran. Achanalt turned out to be a short platform, bare except for a wooden hut set in empty country.

The line had a hungry look about it. It was for all the world like a colonial railway. It was said that the stations were garlanded that week-end. There would not be much to garland. The station buildings were rudimentary, consisting of no more than a small wooden structure and, in some cases, a meagre waiting shed; platforms were unpaved. All the bridges, even large ones over rivers, were built of timber. Everywhere was evidence of the company's struggle to make ends meet.

An easy run down the right bank of the River Bran brought the train to Achnasheen, 'Field of the Rain', a staging post on the road to Loch Maree and Gairloch, where the new station, such as it was, kept company with an ancient coaching inn. From there the travellers faced an hour-long run down the whole length of Glen Carron to Strathcarron.

The train left Achnasheen climbing on the last lap of the climb to the watershed at Luib 646ft above sea level passing on the way a succession of lochs set like jewels in their own mountain basins. First came Loch Gowan and then Loch Sgamhain – Loch of the Lungs. In Loch Sgamhain lurked a water kelpie. It was well known in these parts that it devoured whole anybody unlucky to fall in – except the victim's lungs which floated to the surface. On one side of the train Carn Breac rose to 2220ft and on the other Moruisg frowned down from 3026ft. Down the glen through the Glencarron Woods and past Loch Dughaill, with the River Carron never far away, rattled the little train, constantly surprising the passengers with the vistas that swept past the carriage windows.

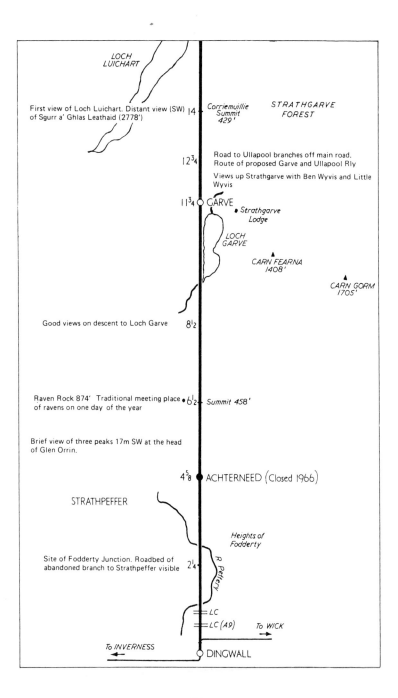

LOCH
LUICHART

First view of Loch Luichart. Distant view (SW) 14
of Sgurr a' Ghlas Leathaid (2778')

Corriemuillie
Summit
429'

STRATHGARVE
FOREST

12¾
Road to Ullapool branches off main road.
Route of proposed Garve and Ullapool Rly

Views up Strathgarve with Ben Wyvis and Little
Wyvis

11¾ ○ GARVE

● Strathgarve
Lodge

LOCH
GARVE

▲
CARN FEARNA
1408'

▲
CARN GORM
1705'

Good views on descent to Loch Garve 8½

Raven Rock 874' Traditional meeting place ● 6½ Summit 458'
of ravens on one day of the year

Brief view of three peaks 17m SW at the head
of Glen Orrin.

4⅝ ● ACHTERNEED (Closed 1966)

STRATHPEFFER

Heights of
Fodderty

Site of Fodderty Junction. Roadbed of
abandoned branch to Strathpeffer visible 2¼

R. Peffery

≡ LC
≡ LC (A9)   To WICK

To INVERNESS   ○ DINGWALL

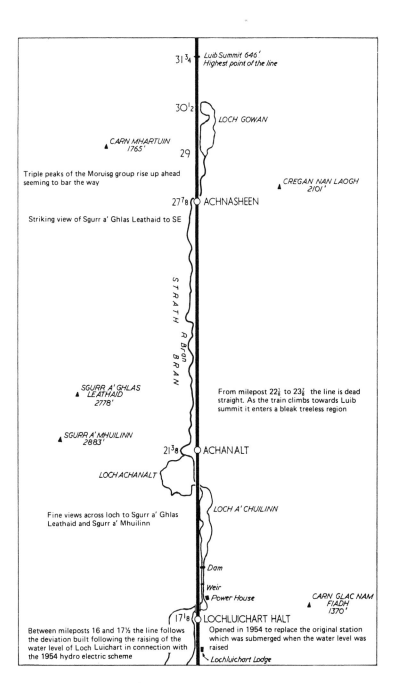

$31\frac{3}{4}$ — *Luib Summit 646'*
Highest point of the line

$30\frac{1}{2}$ — *LOCH GOWAN*

▲ *CARN MHARTUIN*
1765'

29

Triple peaks of the Moruisg group rise up ahead
seeming to bar the way

▲ *CREGAN NAN LAOGH*
2101'

$27\frac{7}{8}$ ○ ACHNASHEEN

Striking view of Sgurr a' Ghlas Leathaid to SE

STRATH
R Bran
BRAN

▲ *SGURR A' GHLAS*
LEATHAID
2778'

From milepost $22\frac{1}{8}$ to $23\frac{7}{8}$ the line is dead
straight. As the train climbs towards Luib
summit it enters a bleak treeless region

▲ *SGURR A' MHUILINN*
2883'

$21\frac{3}{8}$ ○ ACHANALT

LOCH ACHANALT

LOCH A' CHUILINN

Fine views across loch to Sgurr a' Ghlas
Leathaid and Sgurr a' Mhuilinn

Dam

Weir
Power House

▲ *CARN GLAC NAM*
FIADH
1370'

$17\frac{1}{8}$ ○ LOCHLUICHART HALT

Between mileposts 16 and 17½ the line follows
the deviation built following the raising of the
water level of Loch Luichart in connection with
the 1954 hydro electric scheme

Opened in 1954 to replace the original station
which was submerged when the water level was
raised

Lochluichart Lodge

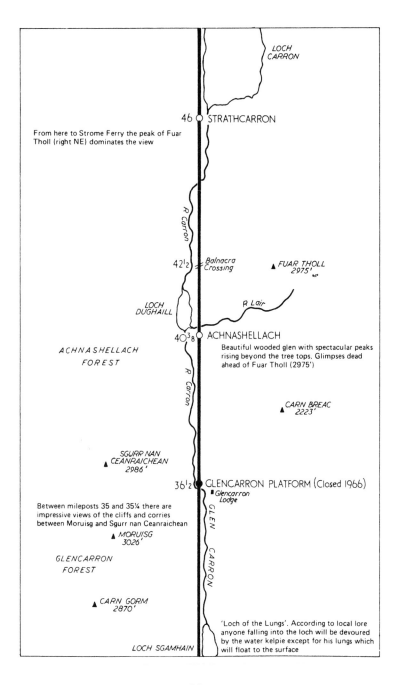

LOCH CARRON

46 STRATHCARRON

From here to Strome Ferry the peak of Fuar Tholl (right NE) dominates the view

R Carron

42½ Balnacra Crossing

▲ FUAR THOLL 2975'

LOCH DUGHAILL

R Làir

40⅜ ACHNASHELLACH

ACHNASHELLACH FOREST

Beautiful wooded glen with spectacular peaks rising beyond the tree tops. Glimpses dead ahead of Fuar Tholl (2975')

R Carron

▲ CARN BREAC 2223'

SGURR NAN CEANRAICHEAN 2986'

36½ GLENCARRON PLATFORM (Closed 1966)

▪ Glencarron Lodge

Between mileposts 35 and 35¼ there are impressive views of the cliffs and corries between Moruisg and Sgurr nan Ceanraichean

▲ MORUISG 3026'

GLEN CARRON

GLENCARRON FOREST

▲ CARN GORM 2870'

'Loch of the Lungs'. According to local lore anyone falling into the loch will be devoured by the water kelpie except for his lungs which will float to the surface

LOCH SGAMHAIN

38

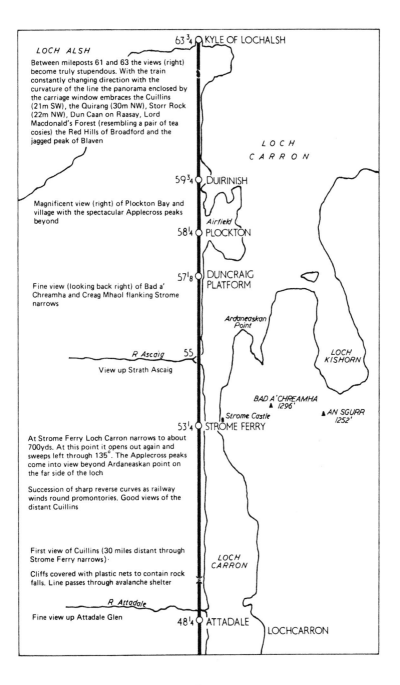

$63\frac{3}{4}$ ○ KYLE OF LOCHALSH

LOCH ALSH

Between mileposts 61 and 63 the views (right) become truly stupendous. With the train constantly changing direction with the curvature of the line the panorama enclosed by the carriage window embraces the Cuillins (21m SW), the Quirang (30m NW), Storr Rock (22m NW), Dun Caan on Raasay, Lord Macdonald's Forest (resembling a pair of tea cosies) the Red Hills of Broadford and the jagged peak of Blaven

LOCH CARRON

$59\frac{3}{4}$ ○ DUIRINISH

Magnificent view (right) of Plockton Bay and village with the spectacular Applecross peaks beyond

Airfield

$58\frac{1}{4}$ ○ PLOCKTON

$57\frac{1}{8}$ ○ DUNCRAIG PLATFORM

Fine view (looking back right) of Bad a' Chreamha and Creag Mhaol flanking Strome narrows

Ardaneaskan Point

R Ascaig 55

View up Strath Ascaig

LOCH KISHORN

BAD A'CHREAMHA
▲ *1296'*

▲ *AN SGURR 1252'*

Strome Castle

$53\frac{1}{4}$ ○ STROME FERRY

At Strome Ferry Loch Carron narrows to about 700yds. At this point it opens out again and sweeps left through 135°. The Applecross peaks come into view beyond Ardaneaskan point on the far side of the loch

Succession of sharp reverse curves as railway winds round promontories. Good views of the distant Cuillins

First view of Cuillins (30 miles distant through Strome Ferry narrows)·

Cliffs covered with plastic nets to contain rock falls. Line passes through avalanche shelter

LOCH CARRON

R Attadale

Fine view up Attadale Glen

$48\frac{1}{4}$ ○ ATTADALE

LOCHCARRON

39

Then, at the end of glen came Strathcarron the last station on the line but one and the climax of the journey. The salt water of Loch Carron, the goal of the Dingwall & Skye promoters for six years, lay ahead. The train wound slowly round the contours of the loch shore, so close to the loch itself that a passenger could have dropped a stone into the water, while on the left of the track a curtain of rock rose high above the carriages. The passengers were unlikely to complain that the train took 30min to cover the last seven magical miles. At the end of the line came Strome Ferry pier with *Oscar* waiting alongside ready to depart for Portree, and the Cuillins of Skye forming a magnificent backdrop in the west.

THE FISHERS' BOATS

It is doubtful if many passengers in the train that first day noticed during the stop at Garve that there was an unusually large gap between the up and down set of rails in the station area, and probably no one knew the significance of the gap. To company officials it was a reminder that the Skye line had gone into business without implementing its grandest scheme.

The directors had planned to carry not only fish but *fishing boats* across Scotland between the eastern and western seas. The idea was that the vessels would sail up the Dingwall canal to a wharf specially constructed alongside the railway. They would then be lifted out of the water, placed on trucks built for the purpose, conveyed across country to Strome Ferry and lowered into the water.

The scheme had great potential. The east coast fishing fleet regularly went to the west coast fishing grounds. They were sailing boats and the voyage round the north of Scotland was long and could be dangerous. The alternative route through the Caledonian Canal was safer and quicker but it was expensive and the fishermen were still faced with the long haul from the western end of the canal to the fishing grounds. A new route that would usurp the function of the canal or eliminate the time-wasting and dangerous circuit of the north of Scotland was bound to find favour with the fishermen. The scheme was no pipedream. The special boat trucks were designed, the cranes ordered and the line engineered to take into account the overhang of the boats while in transit.

The story is told in a series of minute book entries under the heading 'Fishers' Boats' and in correspondence between Murdoch Paterson, William Stroudley (locomotive superintendent of the Highland Railway), Andrew Dougall and others. During the summer of 1869 Paterson re-examined the line with the passage of boat wagons in mind. In a report to the board on 26 June he stated, 'In order to admit of the fishing boats which are 16 feet wide being conveyed between the east and the west coast it will be necessary to slope the rock cuttings at two or three points on the line.' Paterson was asked to furnish an estimate of the cost of doing this.

By 13 September the engineer was in a position to write to Stroudley:

I shall feel much obliged by your sending me at your earliest convenience a section showing a fishing boat on wagons in order that I may have the rock cuttings and the road bridge at Garve widened to suit. At the passing places I propose to make a 10 feet space between the lines in order that a train of boats may pass safely a passenger or goods train.

On 6 December Paterson was again writing to Stroudley:

Mr Dougall tells me you have tracings of the 15-ton cranes for lifting or lowering the fishing boats. He wishes me to look at them as he is to bring the subject before the board at eleven tomorrow. If you are in possession of the tracings perhaps you will be good enough to send them to me by the bearer and oblige.

Paterson got the information he sought and duly informed Dougall:

I received yesterday from Mr Stroudley drawings and tracings of three different cranes for loading and unloading fishing boats at Dingwall and Strome. The drawings represent cranes capable of lifting 15 tons and the offers for them are as follows.

Forrest & Barr, Glasgow	£235
Cowans Sheldon & Co Carlisle	£250
P & W McLellan, Glasgow	£260

Paterson continued:

I examined the drawings carefully and although details are wanting I think that Cowans & Sheldon's is the best. As regards the price £250 for each crane appears too high, and I showed the drawing to Mr Falconer who thinks that £200 is the proper charge and that any little fittings necessary for making the crane at Strome suitable as a 5-ton crane for general purposes should go for nothing.

On 4 March 1870 the company ordered two boat cranes at £243 each and three warehouse cranes at £24 from Cowans Sheldon. It was hoped that the railway would be opened and the cranes installed for the early summer migration of the fishing fleets, but that was not to be. When it became plain that a July opening was the best that could be hoped for Paterson on 8 March informed Cowans Sheldon:

As the two 15-ton cranes for loading fishing boats will not be required this year nor before April or May next please stop further progress with them in the meantime as the directors do not wish to pay for them until required.

That was the last that was heard of the 'fishers' boats' episode. Bogged down by financial and operating worries the Dingwall & Skye allowed its imaginative scheme to lapse. The '10-foot-way' at Garve remained as a monument to the brave venture.

EARLY DAYS

The Skye line had a good summer. Between 19 and 28 August the trains earned £719 1s 2d, then in one exhilarating week in September the revenue climbed to £519 10s 0d. The directors were jubilant. But there were danger signs. Strome pier was found to be bulging at both ends and required £1000 to put it right. A sudden storm damaged the station buildings to the extent of £25.

It was when the tourists and curiosity seekers departed and the families left the big houses for their winter retreats that it was brought home to the board what was involved in working a Highland railway. The trains ran nearly empty. From 1 November the service was reduced to only one train a day from Dingwall to Strome Ferry and back. All winter the solitary train with at the most three carriages and eleven goods wagons rumbled over the empty miles. It was more than enough to cope with the traffic offered. There was a disastrous week in December when it earned only £89 – less than 2s 10d a mile, a scant reward for the money and effort expended in building the line.

The company's shipping venture proved a fiasco. The initial service provided was grossly extravagant, and soon was cut to three weekly sailings to Portree and one to Stornoway. Within a few weeks *Oscar* was wrecked and written off and the Stornoway call abandoned. *Jura* proved unreliable in service, sometimes missing the train connection at Strome on the inward journey. A notice in the timetable saying that on such occasions passengers should travel by the next available train (which more than likely was next day) did not encourage travellers to use the route. Shippers proved impervious to the blandishments of Dingwall & Skye canvassers deployed in the islands and continued to send the bulk of their general cargo by the well-tried Hutcheson service direct to Glasgow. The company was more successful with the fish merchants to whom the new quick route to London was a boon.

The second train was restored in the winter of 1871–2 with a departure from Strome Ferry at 8.30am. A fish merchant by the name of Barbour insisted that the timing was wrong and that it would be of better service if it left Strome at 5.45am. Eager to please the board altered the time, but at the next meeting the train was reported as 'carrying no fish and scarcely any passengers.' The old timing was restored and Barbour was informed that he would get a train at 5.45am if he guaranteed a paying load.

After two years of operation the pattern of traffic on the line began to emerge. In the first complete year a quarter of the total number of passengers travelled first class, an unusually high proportion compared with other lines. The figures were 1st class 10,561, 2nd class 1556, and 3rd class 42,944 yielding £2084 14s 1d, £311 13s 2d and £4625 19s 11d respectively. In the second year the total number of passengers increased from the first year's 55,061 to 63,010 the division between the classes remaining proportionate – 1st class 12,352, 2nd class 1733 and

3rd class 48,925 yielding £2383 9s 0d, £341 4s 9d and £5400 6s 3d. The Dingwall & Skye was predominantly a passenger line. In the year ending August 1871 the company derived £7786 9s 4d from passengers and £3403 10s 4d from freight. The corresponding figures in the second year were £10,013 10s 2d and £4269 10s 8d. Since a high proportion of the passengers were tourists it followed that there was a wide difference in revenue between the summer and winter months. In a typical year the line's total revenue for August was £2871 and for December £770.

On 29 December 1872 the Highland and Dingwall & Skye boards met separately in Inverness. Alexander Matheson chaired both meetings. His theme was that the English were discovering Scotland and were going there instead of to Germany and Switzerland. He spoke of tourists in increasing numbers finding their way to Wester Ross and Skye and returning to tell their southern friends of the glories of these hitherto inaccessible regions. Matheson emphasised that Portree needed five times the existing hotel accommodation. 'What I would like to see there,' he said, 'would be a hotel equal in size to those we meet with on the Rhine and in Switzerland occupying as much space as one side of the main street of Portree.'

Life was tough for men on the Skye line. Few of the cottages that had been promised for the staff had materialised and those that had were small stone boxes with neither drainage nor piped water, not that there was anything remarkable about that in those parts. A stationmaster who had the temerity to ask for running water to be piped to his house was told that there was plenty of good clear water running in a stream 150yd up the line. Even Strome Ferry had to make do with a single unpaved platform with one timber shed – a far cry from the prestigious western terminal planned for Attadale. The engine shed water tank was of wood the company being unable to afford iron.

Staff, including stationmasters, were expected to find accommodation where they could. The stationmaster at Strathpeffer reported that he could find no shelter for his family and himself in the district at a price he could afford to pay. Three years after the line was opened a house was built for him *and* a water supply piped to it from the Saint's Well although adjacent Achterneed village was not to enjoy the luxury of piped water until 1912. Achanalt had to wait for more than a year before it got even a waiting shed.

In the entire length of the line there was not a single surfaceman's cottage although the men were expected to patrol their long exposed sections daily in all weathers. They carried their food with them and found shelter where they could. It is said that they lived like tinkers. It was not until October 1872 that seven double cottages were authorised – near the viaduct at Achanalt, at Achnasheen, Luib summit, Glencarron, Attadale and near the crossing of the Blackwater.

Achnasheen was a special case. The old-established inn there had expected the railway to give it a new lease of life. But Mr Matheson MP, good businessman that he was, applied to the company for a feu of ground at the station for the construction of refreshment rooms. Travellers arriving by train and intending to take the road to Loch Maree and Gairloch it was hoped would fortify themselves for the journey at the station rather than at the old inn. On the somewhat specious grounds that the inn, after all, was 800yd from the station Matheson was granted his feu. The refreshment room blossomed into a substantial hotel which had its front door opening on to the station platform and not on the adjacent public highway.

Once the hostile landowners had accepted the railway as a fait accompli they applied their wits to extracting the maximum personal benefit from the facility they had tried to stifle at birth. Some of them wanted private stations while others concentrated on influencing the siting of public stations to suit their own interests rather than the interests of the public. There were three private stations – Lochluichart between Garve and Achanalt, Glencarron and Achnashellach between Achnasheen and Strathcarron. Some of the public stations were virtually private stations depending for most of their traffic on the comings and goings of the local landed proprietor. All the private stations eventually entered the timetable as public stations.

Shaw of Glencarron, who so recently had barred the contractor from his lands, offered to purchase £1000 worth of shares and permit the company to build a private station near, but not too near, his mansion. The Dingwall & Skye replied that it would allow Mr Shaw to build a private station at his own expense provided he took £2000 worth of stock. The station, like so many structures on the line, failed to appear by opening day. Shaw wrote from his winter quarters in the south to ask when his 'accommodation' would be ready and was told that work on it would begin when the weather improved. Shaw also demanded an 'allowance' because the line, where it passed along the shore of Loch Sgamhain in his territory had been fenced only on the landward side, an economy measure that had seemed natural to the impecunious railway proprietors.

It was not until the spring of 1872 that Shaw got his station – the usual short, bare platform – and a notice was issued to the staff explaining how the platform was to be worked:

Please note that we have agreed to stop all ordinary trains run over the Dingwall & Skye Railway at Glencarron platform either by signal, or by notice given at Achnasheen or Strathcarron stations, as the case may be, for the purpose of setting down or picking up the Proprietor or any member of his Family, Visitors or servants; also for all Parcels or Van Goods belonging thereto which can be taken off or put into a vehicle by the guard.

That routine Dingwall & Skye Railway notice is in a way a social document. Nobody then, including its compiler, would have thought it odd to inscribe Proprietor, Family and Visitors, Parcels and Van Goods in capitals and servants in lower case type. Special fares of 1s 5d, 1s 1d and 8½d, first, second and third class respectively, were charged from Glencarron to Achnasheen, the corresponding fares to Strathcarron being 1s 7d, 1s 2d and 9½d. Packages of up to 1cwt were conveyed from Glencarron to Achnasheen for 2d and to Strathcarron for 3d. Mailbags, which were thrown out of moving trains as they passed through, were delivered for 2d.

In the last stages of the construction of the line Lady Ashburton suffered annoyance when Granger's engine *Lochluichart*, named after her estate, set fire to her heather. The good lady sought interdict to prohibit the use of the offending locomotive until it was altered 'so as to prevent the emission of sparks.' The company and the contractor paid for the burned heather between them.

Lady Ashburton was given a private platform within the grounds of Lochluichart Lodge. This annoyed the few ordinary members of the public in the vicinity who petitioned for a public station to be built at the Mossford Road, a little to the west of the private platform. The board decided that whatever accommodation was provided must be made available to the general public. By an agreement signed on 26 April 1872 Lady Ashburton not only relinquished her private platform, but gave the ground for a public station free of charge and contributed £100 towards its cost.

Less accommodating was Tennant of Achnashellach who still owed £4000 in unpaid shares. When he was given a private station the Dingwall & Skye proposed to charge passengers using it a surcharge equivalent to five miles. Tennant indignantly retorted, 'I and my friends will decline to pay more than the legal fare as charged to other passengers for the distance actually travelled and leave the company to take its own course to recover the excess.' The board sent a copy of the agreement to Mr Reay, secretary of the London & North Western Railway, for an opinion. Reay replied that in his view the Dingwall & Skye was *not* entitled to charge the rates quoted.

Within a month of the opening of the line Tennant, taking advantage of the new means of communication, staged an elaborate house party at Achnashellach. Two special trains were required to convey the guests from Dingwall to Tennant's private station. The normal charter fee for a special was 8s per mile. This Tennant refused to pay, but he stated his willingness to pay any reasonable charge decided on by the directors. The board reduced the charge to 4s per mile 'holding this as a special case but intimating to him that for any special trains run in future no deduction from the usual charge will be allowed.'

It was a grand party. It was said that 200 guests travelled on the special trains. But when it was over Tennant refused to pay the specially reduced charge claiming that it was still too high. The board reduced the fare to 1s 10d per mile which was the fee paid by the Skye company to the Highland for the hire of the trains. On that basis each traveller was getting almost 10 miles of travel for a penny. Tennant refused to pay even that modest amount. Two years later, at a board meeting on 5 August 1873 Andrew Dougall reported that 'Mr Tennant has not yet paid for the two special trains run for him in 1871'. It was resolved to adhere to the modified charge intimated to him shortly after the trains were run. But by then Tennant had left the district. There is no evidence in the company's records that the charter fee was ever paid.

Achnashellach station was manned only during the summer months. It had neither office nor living accommodation. It was not until 1 September 1874 that the board resolved 'to request Mr Wilson (who had succeeded Murdoch Paterson as engineer) to prepare a plan and procure estimates of a suitable office at Achnashellach and to contain sleeping accommodation for the stationmaster who is there three months of the year'. The stationmaster spent a summer sleeping in the booking office but in February 1876 he was promised a two-roomed cottage which was to cost £110. When the board saw the plans they instructed the engineer to add a third room at one end of the building. This uncharacteristic burst of squandermania was occasioned by the fact that the board expected the new resident at Achnashellach, Sir Ivor Guest, to make a contribution towards the cost of the improvements. When Sir Ivor refused to part with his money the scheme for the cottage fell through and 'it was resolved to instruct the engineer to limit the expenditure to a wooden erection consisting of an office and small waiting shed to cost £40 to £50'.

In 1873 a platform was provided at Attadale. Nominally a public platform it was used mainly by the family of Mr Matheson MP on whose estate it was situated. Passengers could stop the trains by signalling from the platform to the driver or by giving notice to the guard. Fares were charged to Strome Ferry for passengers travelling west and to Strathcarron for passengers travelling east. Parcels capable of being handled by the guard

Above: Arrival of the first train at Kyle of Lochalsh, 2 November 1897.
J. Templeton collection
Below: MacBrayne steamers at Kyle of Lochalsh pier, 2 November 1897.
J. Templeton collection

Above: Kyle of Lochalsh in the mid 1970s backed by the Isle of Skye. A class 27 diesel locomotive waits to leave with the late afternoon train to Inverness. *P. J. Fowler*
Below: PS *Carham* at Strome Ferry in the 1870s. *Graham E. Langmuir*

without mechanical aid were accepted for conveyance to Attadale but were delivered only if someone was waiting on the platform to sign the waybill.

On 1 March 1878 a siding was opened at Attadale with the
points facing east. There was only one train a day on the line at
the time, the guard of which was given permanent possession of
the siding keys and sole responsibility for operating the siding.

Time tended to stand still on the Skye line. Before the railway
came the scattered inhabitants of those barren acres did not feel
themselves bound to the discipline of the clock, and the habit
persisted after the coming of the railway. The guard of the first
down train of the day, who was presumed to have checked his
watch by the clock at Dingwall station gave the time to stationmasters at every stop and the rules required them to set their
station clocks *instantly*. That was the theory. When it was seen
to work indifferently in practice, and circulars headed 'Lack of
Uniform Time at Stations' yielded no significant improvement,
the company applied a new system of time checks in 1871. At
8.59 every morning the Highland telegraph clerk at Inverness
transmitted the word TIME to all stations. At precisely 9.00am
the line was disconnected for a few seconds and during the
silence stationmasters were expected to set their clocks.

The timetables of the connecting steamers were engagingly
non-committal. A note in the Highland Railway timetable of
1878 read:

> Strome Ferry, Portree and Stornoway. Leaves Strome Ferry every
> Wednesday not earlier than 2.30pm, Portree about 6.30pm reaching
> Stornoway about 1.30am on Thursdays except the fourth Thursday in
> February on which date the steamer will reach Stornoway about 10.0am.

The wanderings of the once-a-month sailing to Aultbea were
described thus:

> Leave Strome Ferry the fourth Wednesday of February not earlier than
> 2.30pm, Portree about 6.30pm, Gairloch about 9.30pm and Aultbea
> about midnight, reaching Poolewe about 1.30am the following day and
> Stornoway about 10.0am.

The company made strenuous efforts to attract the fish traffic. During the herring season almost every train conveyed

loaded fish trucks and it occasionally ran special fish trains. In April 1874 one of the company's agents reported that there was a prospect of the steamers which usually ran from Lochmaddy to Ardrossan and Liverpool using Strome during the fishing season due to start on 15 May. Andrew Dougall took steps to lure the vessels to Strome. A cast iron fresh water pipe was put in to supply the vessels, and a new siding was laid down to speed up handling. Best of all, a powerful steam crane was ordered from G Russell & Company and erected in time for the May traffic. The secretary duly reported that the crane 'was found to be of great service in unloading the steamers'.

At the same time services to the trade were improved generally. Strome platform was paved with 3in Caithness flags. Hitherto the fish merchants had been obliged to leave their fish boxes on the pier all winter and their condition had deteriorated. A Lowestoft dealer proposed that if the Dingwall & Skye built a box store he would be willing to pay a rental equal to 5 per cent of the capital cost of the building. The company built the store and charged 7 per cent as rental.

On the Highland Railway a daily census of passenger stock was made; at the end of the day stationmasters reported to Inverness the numbers of all carriages standing within their station limits. This rule applied also to the Skye line. For the duration of the herring season fish trucks were classed as passenger vehicles for administrative purposes. A typical circular dispatched to stationmasters read: 'During the months of March, May, June, July, August and November the above vehicles (fish trucks) are to be considered strictly passenger plant and reported daily as such. In no case during these months are these wagons to be used for goods traffic without authority'.

The Dingwall & Skye and Highland Railway jointly operated an interesting public relations scheme. Timber merchants in Inverness periodically held timber sales to which they invited builders, joiners and dealers. In December 1873, for instance, when Morrison & Company issued invitations to interested parties along the Skye line the railway company let it be known that anyone presenting an invitation card at any station would receive a free day ticket to Inverness valid for return on the following day. Booking clerks were instructed to mark such tickets 'Wood Sales.' That the fares were a charge on the goods department suggested that the ticket holders were expected to consign their purchases by rail.

THE SKYE BOGIES

In a way the opening of the Skye line decided the future career of William Stroudley who had been locomotive superintendent of the Highland Railway since 1865. In December 1869, while Stroudley was involved in the affair of the fishers' boats, he asked leave from the Highland board to apply for the post of locomotive superintendent of the London Brighton & South Coast Railway. Stroudley was happy at Inverness and apparently had no great desire to leave. He informed the board that he would be prepared to stay if his salary was increased on the opening of the Skye line. The board replied, 'On the opening of the Skye line the salaries of the principal officers, including that of the locomotive superintendent, will be reconsidered.' Dissatisfied with this vague promise Stroudley departed for Brighton. It was David Jones who had to grapple with the motive power problems of the new railway.

The peculiarities of the Skye line called for a special class of engine to cope with them, but this fact did not sink in for some years. Certainly, in 1870, the Highland Railway had no intention of designing a new engine for the line. Two well-worn 2-4-0s from a batch built in 1858 were delegated to work the railway, one being stationed at Dingwall and the other at Strome where a small wooden engine shed was provided. The engines, introduced by William Barclay, locomotive superintendent of the Inverness & Aberdeen Junction Railway as goods engines, and built by Hawthorn of Leith, had 17in by 22in cylinders and 6ft 1½in driving wheels, and their weight in working order was 31 tons. After the formation of the Highland Railway in 1865 they had been used widely on main line goods trains although in following years they had been superseded on the heaviest trains by a more powerful class of 2-4-0 built by

Sharp Stèwart & Co Ltd in 1863 and 1864.

The Highland was well accustomed to dealing with heavy gradients but a line with steep gradients combined with severe curvature was new in its experience. The problems showed up almost at once. The standard Highland luggage vans had trouble on the curves and two vans had to be modified for use on the line. This in turn led to a shortage of vans on the main line and the construction of two new vans was authorised.

Soon the Skye line 2-4-0s were returning to shed with loose front horns and heated brasses. Both engines paid visits to Lochgorm Works at Inverness, but no matter what was done to them the troubles persisted. Plainly they were not suitable for the Skye line, yet the company had nothing better to offer. David Jones, acutely conscious of the problem, suggested that a bogie engine be designed specially to meet the needs of the Skye line, but the suggestion was rejected on the grounds of expense. The board made it clear that if any 'new' engine was obtained for the line it must be a modification of one of the old engines of which they had a large number.

In November 1870, when the Skye line locomotive troubles first became acute, Jones visited an unspecified London railway 'to ascertain the best means of reducing the wear and tear of engine wheels when running on sharp curves'. Details of Jones's southern visit are scanty, but he mentioned the name of Robert Bridges Adams and it is likely that he investigated the possibilities of the radial axle. On his return to Inverness Jones recommended that 'a lateral motion be introduced into a few of the locomotives of the company at a cost of £10 to £15 each engine'. This recommendation the board accepted. At the same time it approved 'converting No 4 engine, when rebuilding it, into a bogie engine for the Dingwall & Skye line at a cost of £120 including royalty'.

No 4 engine dated back to the dawn of locomotive history in the Highlands. It was ordered by the Inverness & Nairn Railway and built by Hawthorn in 1857. It came north by sea for there was no rail link between north and south then. It was a 2-2-2 tender engine with 15in by 20in cylinders. The driving wheels were 6ft and the carrying wheels 3ft 6in. By 1870 No 4 was not only one of the oldest engines on the system but one of the most decrepit. It was significant that the Highland management should think it a suitable candidate for the Skye line.

But old No 4 was never to get to Strome. The board had second thoughts and ordered it to be scrapped. Its wheels and those of No 3 were used in the rebuilding of their still older sister engines No 1 and No 2 as 2-4-0s. But these engines were not for the Skye line.

A year later Jones had another try. In a letter to the board dated 2 October 1871 he requested 'authority to convert two of the late Inverness & Aberdeen Junction Railway goods engines into bogie engines for the working of the Skye line at a cost of £200 each'. The engines referred to were of course the 2-4-0s working the line. This time Jones was authorised to proceed with his experiment.

No 10 was then lying at Lochgorm in bad condition. It was taken into the shops and emerged in 1873 as a 4-4-0 with a new frame, 17in by 24in cylinders and a Jones-type cab and louvred chimney. It was then the custom on the Highland Railway to name engines as far as possible after places where they normally worked. No 10 had carried the name *Westhall*. For service on the Skye line it was renamed *Duncraig*.

There were teething troubles with the bogie, and when the engine was required to handle a heavy train in poor weather its performance was indifferent. But in average conditions it gave good results, so much so that Jones felt confident in converting a second engine, No 7. It joined its sister engine on the line in 1875. The two engines maintained the service with 2-4-0s helping out when extra traffic was offered (as during the herring season) or when one or other of the bogies had to go to Lochgorm for routine overhaul.

In 1879 Robert Fairlie offered to supply one of his celebrated double engines for the Skye line. He claimed that the engine would not only master the curves and gradients but would prove very useful in getting itself out of snowdrifts, but Jones thought the Fairlie engine unsuitable for Highland conditions.

The Skye line was at a disadvantage in that it had only the two bogie engines. In 1880, when one of the engines was in the shops the traffic manager complained of bad timekeeping on the line, the replacement engine not being up to the job. The board considered the conversion of more 2-4-0s, all of which by then had been partially rebuilt with new cabs and chimneys, and with their cylinder stroke increased to 24in, but with their wheel formation unchanged. Jones vetoed the proposal because of the advanced age of the engines.

In 1874 Jones had designed a 4-4-0 express engine for the Perth-Inverness trains. By 1880 ten of the class were giving excellent service on the principal expresses and the board was thinking of adding to the class. Jones sought permission to adapt one of the proposed 4-4-0s (it was of the 60, or Bruce, class) for service on the Skye line and permission was granted provided that no expense was involved in producing the new design. Using some of the drawings and parts of the earlier class Jones created the Skye bogie. On 4 January 1882 the board announced that the new engine was ready and that three more would be built. But two years were to pass before the first engine, No 70, got a sister.

The Skye bogies became a legend. It was just the type of engine for which the line had been awaiting so long. It had 5ft 3in driving wheels in place of the 6ft 3in wheels of the 60 class and its boiler pressure was 150lb/sq in compared with the 140lb/sq in of the earlier engine and at 43 tons it weighed a ton more. The outside cylinders were 18in by 24in. Eight more engines were built, Nos 85–88 between 1892 and 1895, 5, 6 and 7 between 1897 and 1898 and 48 in 1901. The well-loved little engines, with their wide Crewe-type frames, waddling round the curves like fat, friendly ducks became part of the Ross-shire landscape. They seldom strayed far from the Skye line, although No 48 travelled down to Perth crossed by the Caledonian to Crianlarich and then went up the West Highland to work the Invergarry & Fort Augustus on its opening.

Inexplicably, the Skye bogies were not named. Classes built before and after them were named but not the Skye bogies. It was not the first, nor was it to be the last time that the power in command, whether private or state, was to show a lack of understanding of the Skye line's potential. As a tourist attraction alone named engines would have been worth while. And what a wealth of local place names there was to draw on. Or men who had been associated with the building of the line might have been commemorated in the names of the engines – *MacLeod of MacLeod* or *Sir Alexander Matheson*, but not *Sir William MacKenzie*.

The day-to-day operational hazards were many. From time to time engines stuck on the banks and had to drop back with their trains to a level stretch to get their breath back. The weather could have a marked effect on the running, with wet rails being a particular source of trouble. A peculiarity of the district was that the weather conditions west of Luib summit could be very different from conditions in the east. A daily weather report was telegraphed from Strome Ferry to Dingwall and drivers of down trains were required to lighten their loads if conditions were bad. Even in good weather the permitted load was kept well within the maximum capacity of the locomotive. A standing instruction to station agents read, 'As trains on the Dingwall & Skye line can only take a limited number of vehicles it is necessary to prevent disappointment that agents, before loading live stock to or from stations on this section, ascertain from the superintendent of the line or the respective goods managers whether such can be taken forward'.

It was not unknown for trains to run away. In 1876 Skye line stationmasters were issued with a special notice headed 'Trains on Inclines' and beginning: 'Trains having recently broken asunder descending inclines . . .' Then followed instructions to drivers on how to deal with these distressing occurrences: 'In such cases it is their duty to regulate the speed of the front portion so as to admit of it and the rear or detached portion again coming together GENTLY'.

David Jones kept a Notice Book at Inverness which served the dual purpose of listing operating instructions to drivers and firemen and recording the misdeeds of engine crews, together with the retribution exacted on offenders. If the evidence of the black book is accepted, the behaviour of the Skye line men was all but impeccable. But one cannot help thinking that much that took place between Dingwall and Strome Ferry never

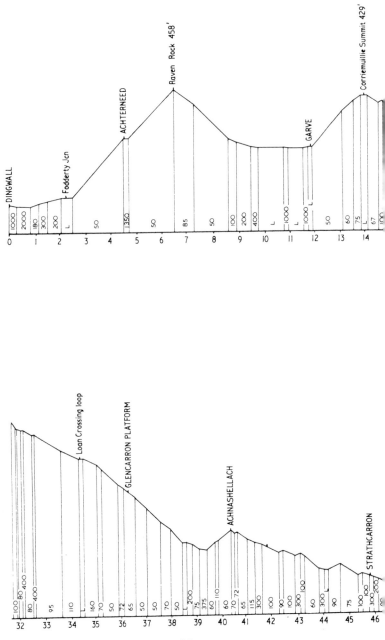

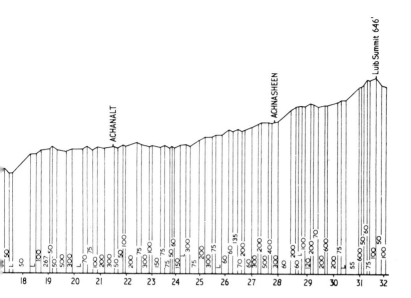

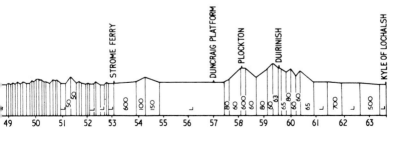

59

reached the ears of the Inverness hierarchy.

Enshrined in the record, however, is the lapse from grace of D. Campbell and D. Finlayson. They were young engine cleaners at Strome. They were first up among the railway community in the mornings. Their job was to light a fire in the engine of the 5.45am up mail train and otherwise prepare it for work, after which they were required to rouse the driver and fireman. On the day of the crime the passengers streamed off the boat to find that their train was without an engine. Campbell and Finlayson had slept in. They were fined 1s 6d each.

Then there was the occasion when Alex Fraser, driver of the morning mixed train, during the stop at Garve went into the station office to exchange gossip with the porter, leaving his fireman John McKenzie to get on with the shunting. McKenzie failed to observe that the points were wrongly set and crashed the engine into a line of stationary wagons. Fines of 10s and 5s were imposed on driver and fireman respectively.

Random entries give fleeting glimpses of Skye line problems. For instance:

> Enginemen on the Skye line are requested to sound the engine whistles as little as possible, especially between Strathpeffer and Dingwall where the road runs close to the line and is much travelled on by horses which are frequently startled by excessive whistling.

> It is reported that a new hosebag which was placed on the Achnasheen water column last month was cut by a knife a few days after having been put there, a piece of wanton mischief for which the protractor will be summarily dismissed if discovered.

> All enginemen passing over the Skye line are hereby cautioned to keep a sharp lookout for signals from surfacemen who are watching for broken rails and dangers from swelling owing to intense frost.

CHAPTER 3

The Steamboat Operation

TROUBLED WATERS

Since the avowed purpose of the Dingwall & Skye Railway was
to serve the Isle of Skye it was right that the directors should
regard the ancient Kyle-Kyleakin ferry as an extension of their
railway. The Act of 1865 empowered the company to acquire or
lease the ferry and employ steam vessels. But it was very specific
about where the vessels were to be deployed: 'The Dingwall &
Skye Railway Company shall use such steam vessels for the
purpose of the said ferry and for no other purpose whatever'.

The Deviation Act of 1868 put paid, for the time being
anyway, to the railway to Kyle of Lochalsh and the requisition
of the ferry. That Act gave the Dingwall & Skye powers to build
a pier *at Attadale*. Nowhere in the statute book is there an Act
empowering the company to build a pier at Strome or to operate steamers from there or anywhere else. Yet a steamer link
with Skye was vital to the success of the railway. Now it was not
just a matter of a ½ mile ferry journey; the Strome Ferry to
Kyleakin run involved a voyage of 15 miles. The directors were
undaunted. They had no more intention of running their own
steamers on the route than they had of running their own locomotives on the railway. It came as a shock to them when their
invitation to David Hutcheson to supply the steamer service
was rejected. Andrew Dougall then advertised in the press for
an operator to run the Skye service. He received no replies.

It was now plain to the board that they would have to establish a shipping line of their own. Only six weeks before the anticipated opening date of the railway a Captain Herd was paid
a fee of £30 to search the Tyne, Humber and Clyde for suitable

vessels. He recommended the purchase of two vessels, *Oscar* and *Jura*, then employed in the Glasgow-Bristol trade by Sloan & Company of Glasgow.

Oscar was built by Denny of Dumbarton in 1850. She was an iron screw steamer of 341 tons. *Jura* too was a Clyde-built iron screw steamer having come from the yard of Wingate & Company as the *Admiral Cator* of the West Hartlepool Screw Steamship Company. The Dingwall & Skye at once paid a deposit of £380 on the vessels, but Sloan & Company refused to accept a bill at six months for half the purchase price of the steamers (£3400) unless signed by a director. Matheson duly signed and work on preparing the vessels for the voyage to Strome was put in hand. *Oscar* arrived on the last Friday in June and *Jura* followed next day. Captain McHardy, who brought in *Oscar* immediately complained of navigational hazards in Loch Carron and advised that dangerous rocks be buoyed without delay. David Jones came down from Inverness to inspect the machinery.

Many of the passengers who came to Strome from the islands were seeing a train for the first time. The trouble was there were too few passengers. The service offered daily sailings to Portree and three sailings weekly to Stornoway, but was absurdly lavish for the traffic available. An experienced ship operator never would have fallen into that trap. The timetable required too much of the ageing vessels and their performance was unreliable.

If the islanders were tardy about patronising the railway boats the same could not be said about the island authorities in their zeal to extract a full pound of flesh from the new enterprise. Stornoway Harbour Commissioners demanded £120 per annum in pier dues. Lord Macdonald wanted a penny per registered ton every time a vessel called at Portree. The schedule required a vessel to make a morning and afternoon visit. This meant that *Oscar* had to pay £16 10s a week for the privilege of calling at Portree, a considerable sum when related to the fact that most of the passengers travelled steerage at 3s for the return trip from Portree to Strome. The Dingwall & Skye directors protested and Lord Macdonald reduced his dues to a more realistic $\frac{1}{2}$d per ton, the morning and afternoon calls to count as one.

With the onset of winter the Stornoway sailing was abandoned and the Portree service reduced to three trips a week. Then on 9 November *Oscar* ran on rocks near Applecross. The newspapers reported her a total loss. Captain McHardy in his official report to the board expressed the opinion that the vessel 'is not likely to be got off in a state to be turned to any useful purpose'. Andrew Dougall was in London at the time of the stranding. The board, unnerved by the incident, instructed Dougall to see David Hutcheson in Glasgow on his way home and try to persuade him to take over the steamboat operation. On 21 November Hutcheson wrote to Dougall:

> Having fully considered the subject you lately brought before us we have come to the conclusion that we could not run a steamer or steamers specially in connection with the trains of the Dingwall & Skye Railway without a serious loss of money and we have therefore resolved not to undertake it. But if there be any way whereby we can work in with the line with our present boat to our mutual advantage we shall be glad to do it.

David Hutcheson had been in the West Highland trade since 1851. Coming from a man of his experience that letter must have been a cold douche to the Dingwall & Skye directors. At least a little was salvaged from the wreck. From 1 December *Jura* on two of her three weekly calls at Portree connected with Hutcheson's Stornoway boat *Clansman*. Dingwall & Skye through tickets to Stornoway, Lochmaddy, Lochinver, Ullapool and Gairloch were accepted on *Clansman*, Hutcheson being paid a mileage proportion by the railway company.

The board reached the conclusion that one steamer would meet all their needs, the smaller the steamer the better. So they decided to get rid of *Jura* and look for another vessel. However, in January Dougall again visited Glasgow in the hope of persuading Hutcheson to acquire *Jura*. He was as obstinate as ever. The reluctant shipowners resigned themselves to the fact that they would have to continue operating their one vessel fleet. Dougall had hardly settled down in Inverness when he was dispatched to the south again, this time to see the chairman of the North British Railway in Edinburgh, concerning that company's steamer *Carham* then plying in the Clyde. But before Dougall went to Edinburgh he called yet again on David Hutcheson in a final attempt to induce him to take over the Strome-Portree service.

Carham was a railway steamer with a history. She was a flush-decked iron paddle steamer of only 159 tons with a single funnel and two masts and was propelled by a double steeple engine. She was built in 1864 by A & J Inglis of Glasgow for NBR Solway services, and named after the country house of the then chairman of the company, Richard Hodgson of Carham Hall. She was transferred to the Tay in 1868 and to the Clyde in the following year, still in the service of the NBR. She plied to the Gareloch (in the Clyde estuary, not to be confused with Gairloch) piers from Helensburgh. In 1870 she had mechanical trouble and was involved in a collision with another vessel. The North British decided to replace her with a modern vessel and *Carham* was put up for sale. To the Dingwall & Skye this small vessel going for a modest price and apparently cheap to operate seemed just right for their purpose. Mr Dallas, a Skye line director, got his friend Napier, the famous Clyde engineer, to inspect *Carham's* hull, engine and boiler. On his recommendation Dougall concluded a deal with the NBR by which he acquired the vessel for £3000.

The last had not been heard of the wrecked *Oscar*. She was not the write-off that the company believed her to be. In the spring of 1871 she was refloated and taken to Glasgow. An underwriter tried to get the Dingwall & Skye to part with the ship's policies for £1000 but Dougall refused to deal with him. Dougall demanded, and eventually got, the full amount of the policies plus interest.

When *Carham* arrived at Strome a Glasgow shipbroker offered to find a buyer for *Jura* at £3750 with five per cent commission for himself. The directors refused the offer and a few days later sold *Jura* themselves for £3500. On the following day *Carham* was damaged at Gairloch but not mortally, and she was soon back in service.

When Alexander Matheson met the shareholders at the

annual meeting in October 1871 he was apologetic about the steamers. Explaining the retreat from Stornoway he said:

> We have ceased to go to distant ports where the traffic was small and inadequate to meet the expenses involved in the long sailings. In short we have gained some experience of steamers which is of value to us, and we know by this time where the valuable traffic is to be got. There is no doubt that we have been somewhat unfortunate with our steamers the first year and I hear it sometimes remarked that it was a pity we did not get new steamers instead of the second hand ones we procured. But the answer to this is – we had not the capital.

The 1872 and 1873 seasons passed uneventfully with little *Carham* paddling from Strome to Portree and back three times a week and occasionally doing special sailings to Gairloch and other places when traffic offered. If the company had hoped to save on pier dues by employing a lighter vessel they were to be disappointed. Lord Macdonald raised the dues at Portree to 2d per registered ton. From January 1872 *Carham* included a call at Plockton in her Portree run. The village four miles down Loch Carron from Strome had been on the route of the railway as originally planned. There was no pier there, but two local boatmen were paid £10 to row passengers to and from the steamer for a six month period. *Carham* was serviced and coaled at Strome, the coal coming from Lanarkshire by rail. MacLeod of MacLeod complained of the expense of this operation and suggested that Portree should be the coaling station with the coal being brought cheaply from Glasgow by sea. There is a record of a vessel *Chieftain's Bride* taking on at Glasgow £60 worth of coal consigned to the Dingwall & Skye Railway at Portree.

Carham did what her undemanding schedule required of her. But she could not cope with special events such as mass sheep movements from Skye, and to deal with such traffic the company had to charter vessels for up to six weeks at a time. Chartering was also resorted to when the vessel was out of action undergoing repairs or periodical Board of Trade tests.

It was when they came to compete for the coveted mail contracts that the board became aware of *Carham's* limitations. The GPO in awarding contracts looked for reliability and frequency of service. The department was not disposed to trust the mails to a vessel that called at Portree only three times a week and not at all at Stornoway. In December 1872 the board decided to give daily sailings to Portree for three months of the year and three weekly sailings for the remainder of the year and won a mail contract worth £1500 – a windfall to the impecunious company. In April 1873 the contract was revised to give £1000 for a basic year-round service of three trips a week with £650 for up to 56 extra trips during the year as required by the Post Office.

By the end of the 1873 season *Carham* was in a bad way; she needed a new boiler, a new funnel, safety valves and steam chest casing. *Carham's* future as a mail boat was very much in doubt. With so much at stake it was imperative that a new vessel be placed on the station as soon as possible, and Dougall was dispatched to Glasgow to search for one. It happened that G & J Burns had a 347 ton iron screw steamer for sale, the *Ferret*. Denny of Dumbarton examined it at Dougall's request and reported favourably. The price asked by Burns was £15,000. The vessel was put into J & G Thomson's yard to have a new cabin fitted at a cost of £1412. Dougall thought he had been 'highly charged' but paid up. *Ferret* arrived at Strome on the first Friday of January 1874 and took up the Portree mail run with the understanding that she would give a once weekly service to Stornoway beginning on 1 May.

Carham was anchored at Portree and 'placed in charge of a suitable man' while the board pondered what to do with her. The directors decided to put her on the Kyleakin, Gairloch, Balmacara, Applecross run, but first they sent her to the Clyde for an overhaul. An extensive refit was carried out by Inglis her original builder at a cost of £4000, but the money was largely wasted for *Carham* was not used again in the regular West Highland passenger trade. During the summer she did an occasional run to Gairloch. She was also seen on the sheep trade and for several weeks during the herring season she was chartered to Stornoway fish merchants. *Ferret* coped with all the winter sailings, which, in addition to the Portree run, eventually included a weekly visit to Stornoway, a fortnightly visit to Gairloch and a monthly visit to Poolewe. The people of Ullapool

Above left: Achnashellach in 1954. *J. Templeton collection*
Above right: Glencarron platform with passenger-operated signals. *J. Templeton*
Below: Garve from the east. The wide space between the up and down lines was
planned to give clearance to fishing boats in transit. *J. Templeton*

Above: One of the 'Skye bogie' 4–4–0 locomotives, designed specially for the Skye line by the Highland Railway and virtually the standard motive power from the 1880s until the first world war. *Locomotive & General Railway Photographs*
Below: Kyle of Lochalsh shed in the 1920s with two Clan Goods 4–6–0s and a small Ben 4–4–0. *Locomotive & General Railway Photographs*

petitioned for a monthly visit from *Ferret*. The Dingwall & Skye offered to send their vessel provided the people of Ullapool signed an agreement to send *all* their traffic via Strome. This condition was unacceptable for it would have meant that Ullapool would have lost the services of the regular Hutcheson boat and of the carrier on the Garve-Ullapool road.

In May 1875 *Carham* was beached at Portree for a Board of Trade inspection and was granted a new certificate. The vessel remained underemployed during that summer and in September she was offered for sale. Inglis, who had carried out the £4000 refit just over a year previously offered £1500 for her. Not surprisingly Dougall rejected the offer. Steel & McCaskill of Greenock offered £5000 but the deal fell through. Since there were no further suitable offers the Dingwall & Skye decided to retain *Carham* until they found a purchaser willing to pay between £5000 and £6000.

The board seemed well pleased with the handling of *Ferret*, for in two successive years Captain Carmichael was given a bonus of £15 'for the satisfactory method in which he has discharged his duties'. However, in 1876 the captain incurred the displeasure of the board. *Ferret* was on charter to convey 200 men of the Highland Light Infantry militia from Tarbert to certain villages on the north shore of Loch Carron at the end of their summer training. Captain Carmichael refused to take the ship into the specified disembarkation points on the grounds that the loch at that point was not charted. Captain Shaw of the HLI complained to the board, and Carmichael was reprimanded. The militiamen were promised a reduction in fares when they went to their 1877 camp.

In spite of *Ferret's* success the steamer accounts made dismal reading. Loss on steamers was a recurring theme in reports to the shareholders. It must have seemed like manna from heaven when at the close of the 1877 season the shareholders learned that their shipping interests were to be acquired.

The Highland Railway was in expansive mood. With its long coastline and railheads in the east, west and north the company decided that it could create a steamer fleet and succeed with it where the Dingwall & Skye had failed. Strome was seen as a key port. The *Highland Railway (Steam Vessels) Act* of 1877 gave the company powers to raise £½m to devote to its steamer enterprise. At last adequate capital was to be applied to West Coast shipping. The Highland took over *Ferret* and *Carham* on 1 September 1877 paying £9850 for one and £3600 for the other. A relieved Dingwall & Skye board received the money on 2 October and used it to reduce some of the heavy loans with which it had been burdened throughout its operational life.

A simple table tells more eloquently than words the story of the Skye line's travail during its seven years as a steamboat operator.

Summary of Steamboat Accounts

	Receipts	Expenses	Loss
1871	£1835 16s 1d	£4417 10s 9d	£2581 14s 8d
1872	£2986 19s 8d	£3546 5s 11d	£559 6s 3d
1873	£3667 13s 2d	£4254 11s 1d	£586 17s 11d
1874	£4778 18s 4d	£4954 16s 3d	£165 17s 11d
1875	£5389 7s 0d	£6699 12s 5d	£1310 5s 5d
1876	£4855 19s 0d	£5334 12s 3d	£478 13s 3d
1877	£4968 17s 11d	£5133 9s 8d	£164 11s 9d

The loss on the steamers over seven years was therefore £5857 7s 2d. The following table gives a breakdown of the distribution of expenditure in the first year of operation.

Wages of crew	£1323 2s 7d
Coal and stores	£1772 13s 2d
Insurance	£404 2s 0d
Repairs	£255 2s 5d
Agencies	£462 12s 4d
Harbour and light dues	£119 14s 11d
Miscellaneous	£79 3s 4d

Such was the Highland's heritage.

Ferret and *Carham* reappeared in 1878 wearing their new colours and ready to play their part in the rejuvenated service. One difficulty under the old regime had been that the steamers were out of service for several days when they went to Stornoway or Glasgow for their routine Board of Trade certificate examinations. The Highland Railway acquired a 31-year lease of 15 poles of the foreshore and seabed at Portree and within this area erected a gridiron on which vessels could be placed for inspection. An early visitor to the gridiron for survey was the Highland Railway flagship *John o' Groat* which had been built to the company's order in Dundee for the Orkney and Shetland service. She sliced through the horizontal beams of the gridiron. The company's engineer was told 'to be guided by the advice of a practical person accustomed to such work before he commences to reconstruct the gridiron'.

It did not take the Highland long to discover that their shipping venture had been a ghastly mistake. Nothing changed, except that the deficits which formerly had decorated the Dingwall & Skye accounts now appeared in the Highland accounts. By April 1879 the board was looking for a smaller boat to replace *John o' Groat* and a buyer for *Carham*. In January 1880 the Aultbea and Gairloch service was surrendered to David MacBrayne who had acquired the business of David Hutcheson & Co. On 6 April it was reported that MacBrayne would relieve the Highland of the entire Strome undertaking not later than 1 May. The railway company thought it wise to retain the steamers in the expectation that the new operator would buy them.

Carham meanwhile had grounded at Raasay pier on 30 March. An underwriter came all the way from London to examine her. He ordered that she be taken to the Clyde 'where the necessary repairs will be executed and the vessel delivered to the company in the same state as she was before the accident or the amount of the policy paid'. Repairs to *Carham* were put in hand.

The agreement between the Highland Railway and David MacBrayne allowed the railway company to retire from the steamboat business on the West Coast on 17 April 1880. From 19 April MacBrayne undertook to provide a daily service from Strome Ferry to Portree calling at Plockton, Broadford, and Raasay during July, August and September, four times weekly during May, June and October and twice weekly for the remainder of the year. Services were also to be provided to Gairloch, Aultbea, Poolewe, Stornoway, Lochmaddy, Tarbert, Lochinver, Ullapool, Kyleakin, Balmacara, Glencloy,

Isleornsay and Armadale. The Highland Railway reserved the right to direct MacBrayne steamers based at Strome on special trips, for instance to convey the militia to their summer camps. Clauses in the agreement bound MacBrayne to employ railway labour at Strome pier and to bunker their vessels only with coal brought to Strome by rail. Provision was made for a once weekly cheap fare from Portree to Glasgow the steamer proportion being 2s 6d. Emigrants proceeding from Portree to Liverpool for embarkation were carried between Portree and Strome for 2s 3d.

But MacBrayne did not want the old Dingwall & Skye steamers. The Highland flagship, which had been displayed with pride at the Inverness Wool Week less than two years before, was sold, the company accepting in part payment 'a first class Spanish house in London'. *Ferret* and *Carham* were sent to the Clyde for disposal. The Bournemouth Steam Packet Company chartered *Carham* for four months at £120 a month for pleasure sailing after which she lay idle for some time before passing to the Ramsgate Steam Ship Company who employed her on cross-English Channel trips. She was scrapped in 1886 having spent her final two years plying for a Liverpool operator. *Ferret*, too, found a charterer in 1880.

THE FATE OF 'FERRET'

On 5 October Andrew Dougall reported to the Highland board that 'Mr George Smith of 14 Brunswick Square, London, through Messrs Greig & Sons the company's shipbrokers, had applied for a charter of *Ferret* for six months from 5th instant at £270 per month for a yachting expedition in the Mediterranean'. Mr Smith's wife, it appeared, was an invalid and her doctor had recommended a cruise. If anybody at Inverness saw something incongruous in *Ferret* in the role of a private yacht he kept his opinion to himself. The prospect of a lucrative charter for their idle ship was very attractive to the board. Mr Smith obviously was a man of substance. His bank references were impeccable, as was a supplementary reference from Henderson & Company, shipbrokers of Gracechurch Street London. The charter was granted. Mr Smith loaded the vessel with stores (including 1000 bottles of fine wines) obtained from a Glasgow ship chandler, paid for them with a three-month bill of exchange and *Ferret* sailed from the Clyde. That was the last the Highland Railway was to see of its vessel.

When the first instalment of the charter fell due and was not forthcoming Dougall wrote to Smith at his London address. The letter was returned addressee unknown. An inquiry to Henderson & Company revealed that no such firm existed. Smith's banker disclosed that while their client had had a substantial balance at the time of the Highland Railway's inquiry his account had shortly afterwards been closed and their late customer's whereabouts were unknown. Meanwhile the Glasgow ship chandler who had provisioned *Ferret* had presented Smith's bill of exchange and it had been repudiated. The Highland directors had to accept the fact that their ship had been stolen.

The board sought the help of Lloyds in tracing the missing vessel. The only information forthcoming was that *Ferret* had been reported passing eastwards through the Straits of Gibraltar on 11 November 1880. Then on 28 January the Board of Trade forwarded to Andrew Dougall a letter received from the Registrar General of Shipping and Seamen stating that *Ferret* was at Malta on 24 January 1881. The Highland at once telegraphed an agent in Malta instructing him to seize the ship unless four months' charter fees amounting to £1080 were paid, only to receive the reply that no vessel by the name of *Ferret* had been in Malta.

During February Dougall made special visits to the Board of Trade in London and to Lloyds seeking news of the ship. None of Lloyds' vigilant agents in scores of ports scattered round the world had caught a glimpse of her. But shortly afterwards came information that wreckage positively identified as having come from *Ferret* had been picked up in the Straits of Gibraltar. A claim for total loss was lodged with the underwriters. The Highland Railway was preparing to write the last chapter in the saga of *Ferret* when on 24 April 1881 a telegram was received stating that *Ferret* had been detained in Melbourne and that

Smith and his associates had been arrested and were being held by the Australian authorities. The company advanced £300 to the appropriate Crown department to have the prisoners brought back to Edinburgh for trial.

But the trial took place in Melbourne where an extraordinary story emerged. From the Clyde *Ferret* had sailed to South Wales where most of the original crew was discharged and fresh hands engaged. The vessel sailed for the Mediterranean and was duly reported passing through the Straits of Gibraltar. On the following night Smith reversed course and slipped back through the Straits into the Atlantic at night without navigation lights. Off Gibraltar he jettisoned two of the ship's lifeboats and other gear bearing the ship's name. By daybreak the funnel colour had been changed and certain superficial alterations made to the vessel's appearance. The name was painted out and a new name *Bentan* was inscribed in its place.

Bentan's first port of call was Santos in Brazil. There Smith went ashore and represented to local shipping agents that the ship was bound from Cape Town to London in ballast and that he was open to receive cargo. He sailed with 3092 bags of coffee consigned to merchants in Marseilles.

Once out of sight of land *Ferret* underwent her second change of identity. A few hours with a paint brush produced *India* bound for Cape Town with a cargo of coffee and documents (forged on a portable printing press) to prove it. In Cape Town Smith sold the coffee for £11000. At this point his grand design began to go wrong. He had hoped to sell the ship as well as the coffee in Cape Town and vanish with his gains. But there were no ready buyers and he could not risk staying for more than a few days in a busy port. Men from the West Highlands were everywhere on the high seas and any one of them might have penetrated the thin disguise of the familiar *Ferret*.

Smith sailed on to Mauritius in search of cargo, but none was on offer. Then he took *Ferret* across the Indian Ocean to Port Albany in Western Australia and when he had no luck there he sailed on to Melbourne. Smith was ashore with Captain Wright and Walker, his purser, seeking a buyer for the ship when the harbour authorities, their suspicions aroused because *India's* fires were kept banked ready for a quick departure went aboard and carried out an inspection. A sheet of Highland Railway note-paper found in the log book gave the game away.

Smith and his accomplices, forewarned of the seizure of the ship dispersed to different parts of Australia but all were caught and brought back to Melbourne for trial. The charges were:

1 Conspiracy to defraud the owners of the *Ferret*, the High-land Railway Company.
2 Conspiracy to defraud intending purchasers of the *Ferret* in Melbourne.
3 Conspiracy to deceive the Commission of Trade and Cus-toms by entering the vessel in a false name under which the vessel could have been sold in that port.

Incredibly, the three were found not guilty of defrauding the Highland Railway, but guilty on the two lesser charges. Smith was sentenced to seven years imprisonment and Wright and Walker to 3½ years each. The men were never called to account for the theft of the vessel nor for the series of frauds on agents and ship chandlers who had provided goods and services in exchange for spurious bills, nor did the Highland ever get its charter fee of £2100. The Highland Railway agent in Mel-bourne sold *Ferret* to the Australian Shipping Company for £8000 and she sailed for many years in the Australian coastal trade.

There was a sequel to the story in August 1883 when four of *Ferret's* original seamen who had taken part in the piratical ven-ture claimed hourly wages from the Highland Railway, the sum of £263 19s 8d having been awarded against the company by the Australian court. The Highland contested the case in London but the Judicial Committee of the Privy Council ordered the company to pay the men the sum claimed.

David MacBrayne put his *Lochiel* on the Strome Ferry-Portree-Stornoway service. At last the Skye line was served by a professional steamboat operator capable of giving a first class service. But the benefit to the Dingwall & Skye company was to be short-lived. It had only a few months left of its separate exist-ence.

CHAPTER 4

In Highland Hands

ECLIPSE

By 1880 it was plain to all concerned that a brave Highland transport venture had failed. That the line was a 'social' success was not in doubt, but it had been unable to pay its way. If there was a single cause that brought about the demise of the Dingwall & Skye it was that it was under capitalised to the extent of £90,000. The shareholders simply did not pay up. Large sums of money had to be borrowed from the banks to finish the line, and finding money to repay the loans and meet interest charges placed an intolerable burden on the board. At the end of the fourth year of operation Matheson told the shareholders: 'It is gratifying to observe that the revenue of the year is sufficient to meet the working expenses and debenture interest with a balance over £510 3s 2d. The position might well have been gratifying for a company with its share capital fully paid up, but the revenue did not come anywhere near meeting the interest charges on the loans. Where money to repay the loans was to come from the board dared not think about.

The directors devoted much of their time to devising the most palatable ways of robbing Peter to pay Paul. At one stage ordinary stock was issued at a premium to pay off part of the loan. It was like trying to fill a bottomless bucket. On 12 October 1872 Dougall was sent to Edinburgh 'to inquire of the banks the lowest terms on which £70,000 can be borrowed for two or three years'. A few months later Dougall, reporting on the bank account, stated that in order to meet the debenture interest due at Whitsunday the sum of £1914 5s 4d was required. It was resolved 'to ask the Caledonian Bank to allow a temporary overdraught to this extent on the usual terms to be repaid as soon as possible out of the receipts after deducting working expenses'. 'On the usual terms' suggested that the Dingwall & Skye begging bowl had been rattled at the doors of the Caledonian Bank more than once. Indeed, the bank was a good friend to the company until it too got into difficulties and the liquidator sent pleading letters to the Skye board asking for a speedy repayment of the borrowed money.

Demands piled up relentlessly. Macdonald the contractor had to wait for a year before he was paid the £80,000 balance of his contract, part of it in a bill of exchange not encashable for another two years, and the rails had been supported for two years on chairs supplied by the Darlington Iron Company before the Dingwall & Skye got round to paying for them. But there were lighter moments. On 2 February 1875 Andrew Dougall produced a promissory note from the Caledonian Bank which had been outstanding since 10 November 1873 and had now been repaid. The cancelled note was ceremonially burned in the presence of the board.

Added to their other worries the directors were called upon to deal with internecine strife. The directors were all personal friends and got on well enough with each other, although John Fowler caused some irritation by what some considered to be excessive interference. (It was said that he caused a row at every board meeting, but that is probably an exaggeration.) Certainly Fowler was a man who liked his own way, and he did not always get it in the Dingwall & Skye boardroom. He was a member of the Highland/Dingwall & Skye committee that supervised the working agreement and when a suggestion of his that the Skye line should employ a traffic canvasser of its own was turned down in favour of a counter-suggestion that the canvasser should be responsible to the West Coast group of companies he resigned his directorship.

In March 1872 Andrew Dougall was surprised to receive from a London legal firm a request to be given access to the minute books and accounts of the Highland/Dingwall & Skye joint committee on behalf of John Fowler, Sir John Stuart (who also had resigned his directorship) and two shareholders, Mr

Tennant and Mr Banks. The request was refused, whereupon
Fowler and his friends formed themselves into a Committee of
Investigation and in due course published a report severely
criticising the efficiency and competence of the joint committee.
Copies of the report were sent to prominent people in the Highlands and published in the local press. A month later the Committee produced a second damning report.

On the day following the publication of the second report the
Skye board met to consider how best to counter the allegations.
A written reply was considered inadequate, legal proceedings
time-wasting and expensive. It was decided to convene a public
meeting in Inverness for Saturday 13 July at which the four
members of the Committee of Investigation would be invited to
face the board in the presence of the press and shareholders and
state their case.

The affair had become a *cause célèbre* in the Highlands and the
forthcoming meeting aroused great interest. Even Alexander
Matheson must have been surprised by the number of people
who turned up to witness what promised to be a fiery confronta-
tion. They were to be disappointed. The Committee of Investigation did not appear. There was no mistaking the anti-Fowler
feeling of the gathering which included the company's bankers
and leading local authority officials. After some preliminary
discussion it was resolved 'that the proceedings adopted by certain shareholders in constituting themselves into a so-called
Committee of Investigation into the affairs of the company in
demanding that the accounts and papers of the company
should be thrown open to the inspection of professional men
unconnected with the company and in publishing in the newspapers charges implying grave imputations upon the board,
appear to this meeting uncalled for, irregular and wholly
unwarranted by anything that has taken place in the adminis-
tration of the company's affairs by the board'.

The resolution was approved without a dissenting vote.
Andrew Munro of Invergordon further proposed 'that the self-
styled committee having failed to attend this meeting in order
to substantiate or withdraw the charges and meet the directors
face to face, this meeting requests the directors not to notice any

further statements that may be made in a similar manner by the same parties'. It was left to Provost Mitchell of Dingwall to express the opinion of all present by proposing 'that the meeting desires to express its confidence in the board by whom the company's affairs have up to the present time been ably and successfully administered'.

And so an ugly incident ended. At least it showed the Skye line directors that they stood in good stead with the community they were trying to serve. About six months later Fowler apologised to the Highland Railway. At their meeting on 7 January 1873 the Highland directors discussed his letter of apology and minuted their opinion that it was inadequate. However, in view of the fact that Fowler had been so thoroughly trounced at the public meeting they concluded that it was unnecessary for them to take further action. Fowler disappeared from the Highland railway scene to re-emerge nearly 20 years later in an interesting new role. By then he was Sir John Fowler, engineer-in-chief of the newly-completed Forth Bridge.

A railway could not live on goodwill alone; traffic was needed and it was not forthcoming in sufficient volume to make the railway viable. The twice daily service was maintained throughout the year until 1875 when the trains that left Dingwall at 8.0 am and Strome at 4.35pm were earning only 8½d a mile which included a 4¼d subsidy from the GPO for carrying the mails. The trains were withdrawn on 15 January 1876 when it was agreed that the future basic service would be one train a day throughout the year with an additional service between 1 May and 1 November. The engine shed at Strome Ferry was closed in winter and the Dingwall engine performed the whole work of the railway. The winter timetable now read as follows:

	Down	Up
Dingwall	10.50 am ↑	5.48 pm
Strathpeffer	11.05 am	5.33 pm
Garve	11.25 am	5.13 pm
Lochluichart	11.40 am	4.53 pm
Achanalt	11.55 am	4.40 pm
Achnasheen	12.15 pm	4.20 pm
Glencarron platform		
Achnashellach	12.50 pm	3.45 pm
Strathcarron	1.05 pm	3.30 pm
Strome Ferry ↓	1.35 pm	3.00 pm

During the promotional stage the Highland Railway did not take a financial interest in the Skye company. But in 1872 £35,000 of Highland money was invested in the Dingwall & Skye, the major company being given two seats on the board. The injection of new money was but a palliative. The grinding burden of debt mounted until in 1880 it stood at £74,000. Although revenue had increased at an average rate of £600 a year for the 10 years in which the company had been operating there was no prospect of the line paying off its liabilities. Amalgamation with the Highland was the only alternative to total closure.

When amalgamation seemed inevitable the Dingwall & Skye directors made a projection of future earnings over the next 10 years first on the basis of the railway continuing as an independent concern and second as an integral part of the Highland Railway.

| | Independent | | Amalgamated | |
	Loss	Surplus	Loss	Surplus
1881	£1300		£100	
1882	£700			£1100
1883	£100			£1700
1884		£500		£2300
1885		£1100		£2900
1886		£1700		£3500
1887		£2300		£4100
1888		£2900		£4700
1889		£3500		£5300
1890		£4100		£5900

The Dingwall & Skye board considered that the Highland would be able to save money by replacing the existing $4\frac{1}{2}$ per cent debentures with 4 per cent debentures and by paying off loans and obtaining new loans at the lower rates that would be available to a large well-established company.

Not all the Highland shareholders shared this view. The Highland had lost heavily in taking over the Dingwall & Skye steamers only three years before and they saw no sense in throwing good money after bad by taking over the ailing railway as well. When the *Dingwall & Skye and Highland Railways (Amalgamation) Bill* went to Westminster in the summer of 1880 it was opposed by 48 Highland shareholders representing £109,355 worth of stock. The Highland had already signed cheques to the value of £40,000 in favour of the Dingwall & Skye but was holding on to them until it was plain that the Bill was safe.

The Bill was dealt with by a select committee of the House of Commons on 20 July. Its sponsors were able to show that in the year ending 31 August 1879, of the £13,155 of traffic passing over the Skye line £12,340 had been through traffic in transit to or from the Highland Railway, leaving only £815 as purely local traffic. It was no use pretending that the Dingwall & Skye was a local line serving a local community. It was a feeder to the Highland, a *de facto* if not a *de jure* branch line of the Highland Railway. The *Dingwall & Skye* and *Highland Railways (Amalgamation) Act* of 2 August 1880 formalised the situation and the Skye line ceased to exist as a separate entity on 1 September 1880. The Highland issued £74,000 worth of debentures to cover the Skye company's debts and gave its shareholders £50 of Highland stock for every £100 of Dingwall & Skye stock.

The change in status made little difference to the passengers using the railway. After all Alexander Matheson was chairman of the Highland and Andrew Dougall its general manager and secretary. The same trains made their leisurely way westward to the sea handled by the same men. For the time being the timetable remained the same as before. The line was seldom mentioned in the board room; it was just the Strome Ferry branch. It was allowed to languish. It was seldom noticed in the company's advertising programme. Yet the line retained its unique character unimpaired, as indeed it was to retain it through much more radical changes of ownership in the years to come.

FISH

The acquisition of the Dingwall & Skye by the Highland almost coincided with the opening of the final phase of the

Callander & Oban Railway on 1 July 1880. For 15 years the C & O had been struggling to reach the sea, and now at last there was a second rail-connected port on the west coast. At first the Highland saw no threat to its trade in the new route; it was too far to the south to be a real menace. The main fishing grounds were within six hours' steaming distance of Strome. From Stornoway to Oban entailed a voyage of 16 hours.

But the Highland had reckoned without John Anderson, secretary and virtually general manager of the Callander & Oban. Anderson was a pugnacious, thrusting Lowlander. He had been assistant general manager of the Edinburgh & Glasgow Railway and when that company was absorbed by the North British in 1865 he did not relish the prospect of playing a minor part in a large company. He applied for the secretaryship of the C & O, then newly promoted. Anderson nursed the Oban line much in the way that Andrew Dougall nursed the Skye line, but while Dougall was responsible for the affairs of most of the railways in the Highlands Anderson was able to devote his entire attention to the C & O. He sold shares round the doors to raise money and as the railway was opened section by section he pursued an aggressive commercial policy. It was not surprising that once the C & O was in Oban the interests of Anderson and Dougall should clash.

Anderson went all out to filch fish traffic away from Strome. A townsman, he knew nothing about fish, but he was at pains to learn all he could about the fish trade and the problems of the traders. There were 8970 men and boys working 2477 boats in the fisheries district of which Strome Ferry was the railhead. Anderson applied himself with zest to convincing the fishermen that it would be to their advantage to switch to Oban.

The Stornoway men were ready to listen to the loquacious Lowlander. In recent years the Skye line and the Highland had used their west coast monopoly unwisely. Handling facilities at Strome had deteriorated. The navigation of Loch Carron especially at night was hazardous and appeals by MacBrayne and the fish merchants to the railway board to provide warning lights at danger points went unheeded. When the Highland had withdrawn its own steamers it had not reduced the through rate for fish consigned from Stornoway to London. The fish merchants had to pay carriers for the Stornoway-Strome passage and they felt they were paying twice over.

Anderson offered at Oban a fine modern pier with ample berthage and a safe approach. There were cranes, auctioneers' stances and brand new offices on the pier readily available to the Stornoway men free of charge. The C & O was geared to send fish to London by the West Coast route in conjunction with the Caledonian and London & North Western railways. The West Coast companies offered an official rate reduction of 5s a ton on fish routed via Oban. Anderson promised the Stornoway merchants a secret rebate not approved by the Railway Clearing House of 10s per ton on herrings and 27s 6d a ton on kippers.

Dealers who tried the new route found that Anderson was as good as his word. The speed of handling and dispatch at Oban was impressive. In spite of the extended voyage from Stornoway cargoes were reaching London two hours before cargoes dispatched from Stornoway at the same time routed via Strome. C & O enterprise and efficiency resulted in a drastic reduction in the tonnage of fish passing over the Skye line. The Highland saw the fish trade so painstakingly built up by the Dingwall & Skye wilting away. During the herring season of 1881 the Lochalsh correspondent of the *Oban Times* observed that the C & O had captured 'virtually all' the traffic.

Andrew Dougall set out to retrieve the situation. With the best of the privately-owned boats plying to Oban it was not easy to find an operator willing to carry fish to Strome. At first MacBrayne agreed to put a vessel exclusively on the Stornoway-Strome fish run from 1 May to 20 June but withdrew from the agreement when it was realised that some of the sailings would be at night. MacBrayne had long been complaining about the dangers of Loch Carron by day; regular night voyages were unthinkable. Belatedly the Highland made arrangements with James Wood of Aberdeen to charter a vessel a month at a cost of £285. On its first voyage it brought only 80 boxes of fish to Strome.

The fish war was short lived. The Highland improved its

services and gradually the lost traffic drifted back to Strome. The port's geographical advantage over Oban was overwhelming, and the 'drawbacks' offered to the trade by Anderson were economically unrealistic. By October 1881 the C & O and the Highland were ready to enter into an interim rate and traffic sharing agreement. Competition remained keen, both sides deploying canvassers in Stornoway and other ports, but the cut-throat atmosphere was removed from the operation.

There remained the vexed question of Loch Carron for the hazardous approach to Strome was a deterrent to its use. In 1883 Stevenson the Edinburgh civil engineer had drawn up a plan for the lighting of Loch Carron which he assured the railway company would make navigation 'comparatively safe and easy.' But the cost of the scheme – £10,000 – was prohibitive. The company petitioned the Commissioners of Northern Lights, the body responsible for most Scottish lighthouses to light Loch Carron, but the Commissioners took the view that since the purpose of the lights was to provide a safe path to the company's pier the company would have to bear the cost. In April 1884 McLeod of Cadboll suggested a modified scheme estimated to cost no more than £500. The most dangerous rocks were charted and buoyed and lighthouses and cottages were established on Cat Island and Man Island. When the work was completed the Highland asked the Commissioners of Northern Lights to take over the maintenance of the installations. The Commissioners employed Stevenson to inspect the lights and although they accepted the engineer's report that the work was well carried out they insisted that their maintenance must remain the responsibility of the railway company.

The measures taken to attract shipping had immediate results. In the year ending 28 February 1886 in addition to special fish trains fish wagons were attached to the 3.0pm up mail on 275 of the 323 days on which it ran.

THE BATTLE OF STROME PIER

Meanwhile there had occurred the bizarre episode that came to be known as the Battle of Strome Pier.

At a Dingwall & Skye board meeting on 15 April 1879 the attention of the directors had been called to a protest by the Free Presbytery of Lochcarron regarding railway staff being employed occasionally at Strome pier on Sunday evenings during the herring fishing season. The 'Wee Frees' were strict Sabbatarians. They did no work on Sundays, did not cook food and had been known to stop their clocks at midnight on Saturday for the ensuing 24 hours. Work performed on Sunday caused them deep offence. The Skye board assured them that in future as little work as possible would be done on the railway on Sundays.

It was a paper promise. The fish traffic was vital. If the company (now the Highland of course) was to make the most of the short herring season it had to provide trains and man Strome pier whenever the fish was offered and that included Sunday. Fish caught on Saturdays did not reach Strome until late that night or early on Sunday morning. If it had to catch the London market on Monday it had to be handled and dispatched on Sunday. Strome became a place of brisk Sunday activity during the season.

By the end of May 1883 the herring fishing was in full swing. There was bad blood between the native west coast men and the seasonal intruders from the east coast, partly because the east coasters were using improved fishing techniques which yielded better catches than the more traditional methods employed by the local men. Relations between the two factions were not helped by the fact that the east coasters had no scruples about dispatching their catches to reach Strome on Sundays.

On Friday 1 June the Stornoway men stayed in port to demonstrate against the intruders. They stayed in port on Saturday too, for catches landed that day would not have been taken to Strome until Monday – too late for the south market. The uninhibited east coast men fished on and as luck would have it the herring shoals were exceptionally rich. Three steamers were required to cope with the east coast men's landings and it was late on Saturday when they sailed from Stornoway bound for Strome.

By 1.0am on Sunday morning the *Lochiel, Talisman* and *Harold* were feeling their way up Loch Carron. Their crews may have wondered why fires were glowing here and there along the shore and in the dark surrounding hills. Watchers in the loch-side fishing and crofting communities knew their significance. From the shadows of both shores boats slipped away to converge in the wake of the steamers as they sailed on towards Strome.

About 20 porters received the vessels at the pier. The steam crane hissed and rattled as fish boxes were swung away from the ships' holds to the wagons of the waiting special train. But not for long. Out of the darkness swooped upwards of 50 men. They swarmed over the pier, attacked the craneman and put the crane out of action. There was much shouting and fists flew. When the porters resorted to removing the boxes from the holds by hand the invaders put their shoulders to the railway wagons and pushed them up the pier away from the ships.

In the course of the night more small boats arrived and by daybreak the pier was held by 150 rioters. All work had ceased. The stationmaster remonstrated with the ringleaders but to no avail. The forces of law in Wester Ross were not organised to meet such an emergency. There was *one* policeman in the area. Normally he was based at Plockton, but he had gone to a market 14 miles away on Saturday and had not returned. When the stationmaster telegraphed a report of the situation to Inverness the Highland superintendent asked the military for 'a detachment of bayonets'. He had to make do with the chief constable of Ross-shire and six constables who were dispatched from Dingwall by special train.

The rioters were undaunted by the appearance of the police. They easily repulsed a combined attack by police and railwaymen some of the railwaymen being roughly handled in the skirmish. For the rest of the day the rioters stood their ground watched from a distance by police and porters. People arriving at Strome for church service – held in the station waiting room by courtesy of the railway company – went into the woods and cut sticks in case their help was needed. At length the chief constable withdrew his men after advising the stationmaster not to attempt any work at the pier meantime. The rioters sang a psalm of victory.

The occupation of the pier continued until midnight. On the stroke of twelve the demonstrators quietly withdrew, and their boats were soon swallowed in the darkness of the loch. It was Monday. The unloading of the fish was resumed. The special left at 4.30am nearly 24 hours late. There were enough boxes left over to fill several trucks and these were attached to the 5.30am up mail.

When the rioters departed one of their number was heard to say that they would be back on the following Sunday with their numbers tripled. During the ensuing week rumour was rife that 2000 men recruited from a wide area would lay siege to Strome on the following Sunday. The threat was taken seriously by the authorities who saw it as an extension of the 'Crofters' War' in which dissatisfied crofters in Skye and elsewhere were holding their crofts in defiance of the authorities.

By Thursday the matter was in the hands of the Home Secretary. Hurried arrangements were made to recruit police from Lowland forces and on Friday night four chief constables and 60 men from Lanarkshire and Perth travelled by the night train to Inverness where they were briefed and joined by men from the local force and from Elgin and Nairn. Eyewitnesses spoke of a train filled with big men in plain clothes passing through Dingwall on Saturday morning. Later in the day, sheriffs, county officials and newspapermen were seen in the mail train passing westward. On Friday morning the War Office ordered the officer in charge of Edinburgh Castle to send four officers and 70 men to Strome. They left Waverley station at 8.30am on Saturday. On Sunday their troop train was held at Fort George outside Inverness ready to leave for Strome on receipt of a telegraph message. The ministers of the three Free Presbyterian congregations in the Loch Carron area, who were in Edinburgh for the annual General Assembly of their church hurried home in the hope of exercising a calming influence on their flocks.

On the Saturday more than 200 men came over the hills from Lochalsh and a like number arrived by boat. In the face of massive police opposition, and in the knowledge that a troop train was standing by they were reduced to staging a sullen, silent demonstration while the transfer of the fish went on unmolested. With the departure of the special train at 8.0am the mob dispersed. The police left by train shortly afterwards, except the Ross detachment who stayed behind to ferret out and apprehend the ringleaders.

Early on Monday morning four men were taken from their beds near Plockton and escorted to Dingwall on the early train. Police combed the crofting villages round the loch and made six more arrests. Women gathered up stones in their aprons and pelted the police as their menfolk were taken away. The prisoners were released on bail and returned in triumph along the Skye line to be greeted as heroes and martyrs at every station.

The episode left a deep-seated, anti-railway feeling in the district. Alexander Matheson took steps to identify those of the rioters who were employed on his estate. They were sacked. Threats were made against the railway and men were posted to guard key structures and telegraph wires. Local people boycotted the railway by sending their goods to the south by the steamers at great inconvenience to themselves. The threatening troop train at Fort George caused particular offence. Wester Ross had long been looked upon as a dependable recruiting area for the army. The Lochcarron Volunteer Artillery Corps of 60 men regarded the troop train as an insult and considered resigning as a body. At the first parade after the 'battle' only four men turned up. At the parade held on 27 June, 22 men reported, but, following an appeal by their popular sergeant all but four men appeared on the next parade.

Police protection was provided at Strome Ferry on four Sundays that June. The Highland saw the resulting extra passenger traffic as a windfall. The board at its meeting on 3 July, acting no doubt in what it considered to be a spirit of magnanimity, resolved to charge the police authorities ½d per mile instead of the normal 1d per mile for police personnel travelling to and from Strome. The Police Commissioners paid up, but thought it odd that they had to pay anything for the conveyance of men whose sole purpose had been the protection of the railway company's property. Later the Highland refunded the fares.

A bustling Kyle of Lochalsh in the days cattle and other freight were still handled, against a backdrop of Skye. It is 14 June 1962 and locomotive No 44978 is running round its special, including the two restored Caledonian coaches. *Colour-Rail*

Above: No 45361 waits at Achnasheen to cross a down service in 1954. A restaurant car was regularly transferred from the lunch-time down to the up train here, often while two goods were also within the station limits. *Jim Jarvis/Colour-Rail*

Below: No 45120 near Plockton with an up train in May 1957. *Neil Sprinks/Colour-Rail*

One of the classic shots of the Kyle line. No 37114 is seen leaving Kyle of Lochalsh with the 1110 for Inverness against the background of Skye on 19 July 1985. *W. A. Sharman*

Above: A Sprinter unit on a trial run passing Craig by Loch Carron on 30 April 1988. *Alan Mitchell*

Below: Locomotive 374414 at Fernaig by Loch Carron with the 1015 from Inverness to Kyle on 30 April 1988. *Alan Mitchell*

The rioters and their supporters fired a parting shot by attempting to prosecute the Highland Railway for alleged breach of an old Scottish Sunday observance law, but the Lord Advocate of Scotland refused to instigate criminal proceedings against the railway.

The following piquant observation on the Strome affair was made by a correspondent to a Scottish paper:

> Whilst in Skye the crofters have been allowed to seize and hold lands and their conduct in doing so has by many been highly extolled, here for doing nothing but seizing a terminus of the Highland Railway and interfering with the traffic the authorities are down on the parties who, in the exercise of their discretion have endeavoured to suit the management of the railway to their own views. If other parts of the Highlands are to be handed over to the crofters why in the world are they not to be allowed to take the Highland Railway, the road and approach to their new possessions, and in their own country?

STRATHPEFFER

By 1880 Strathpeffer had decided that the station on the hill that masqueraded as Strathpeffer served the community badly. The village was blossoming into a prestigious inland resort. It was the age of the spa, and Strathpeffer had mineral waters which the Victorian gentry believed to have curative properties. Hotels were built to house the pilgrims. All that Strathpeffer lacked was a railway to bring them to the brink of the health-giving springs.

The Grim Reaper having disposed of the opposition, the Highland promoted without fuss a branch line to run from the point at which the Dingwall & Skye had been so abruptly deflected into the hills down the gentle slope of the strath to a station on the fringe of the village. On 30 July 1884 the Highland engineer was ordered to prepare plans 'in order that the works may be commenced when the crops are off the ground and the line opened to the public in time for the next summer's traffic'. The redoubtable Granger was given the contract to build the line for £5019 5s and undertook to maintain it for its first three months of operation for £50. It was opened from

Fodderty Junction to Strathpeffer on 3 June 1885. On the same day the existing Strathpeffer station was renamed Achterneed.

In its first year the Strathpeffer branch produced £1609 15s 7d in total revenue. (The whole of the Dingwall & Skye had yielded £9345 3s 7d in its first year.) Revenue steadily built up as genuine invalids, hypochondriacs and the fashionable elite flocked to the resort. The Highland lavished attention on the branch and shamefully neglected the parent line. The Skye railway took on the role of an ageing uncle with a brash young (and very successful) nephew.

By the turn of the century, however, Strathpeffer was becoming disenchanted with the Highland. The hoteliers, and in particular the proprietors of the Spa, complained that the services were not up to modern requirements. It was pointed out that passengers from the south, some of them invalids, suffered discomfort and inconvenience in the last stage of their journey by having to change from the through carriages into antiquated Highland Railway vehicles. The then chairman of the Highland was nothing if not frank on the subject. He warned his board: 'We cannot continue many years longer to expect people to travel in stock which might be good enough for Hottentots but is not good enough for carrying ordinary Christian Scotsmen'.

At a public meeting held in Strathpeffer it was claimed that the failure of the railway to provide a direct service from London, the main reservoir of the spa-conscious public, was hampering the development of the resort, the southerners tending to patronise English and Continental spas. 'It amounts to this,' said an indignant Highland shareholder, 'that the travelling facilities from London make or mar a health resort.' He thought a few carriages prominently labelled 'London-Strathpeffer' would do the trick.

Prodded by the Spa proprietors the Highland embarked on a bold publicity venture. The company purchased a 16hp motor car from the Albion Motor Car Company of Glasgow, had it specially painted and embellished with advertising matter and prepared to send it on a tour of England. Local authorities, coach and steamer operators and hotel and shop keepers in the

Highland area were invited to support the enterprise with cash contributions. Sad to relate in the whole area north of Inverness the only support came from the Spa proprietors. No single body public or private, and no proprietor along the Skye line or among the islands it served and whose attractions the motor car was designed to extol, considered it worth their while to participate in the scheme.

The Highland Railway motor car made its first safari into England in 1908 when it visited Carlisle, Preston, Liverpool, Manchester, Salford, Oldham, Rochdale, Burnley, Halifax, Dewsbury, Sheffield, Leeds, York, Darlington, Hartlepool, Sunderland and Newcastle. The car, with its headboard inviting the lieges to stop it and ask for information certainly aroused English curiosity about the Highlands and especially about Strathpeffer. The *Newcastle Daily Journal* of 18 May advertised an excursion from Newcastle and Sunderland to Strathpeffer and the Skye line. A team of English journalists travelled north to see for themselves what the Highland Railway had to offer. An English writer called Strathpeffer 'the sanatorium of the British Isles', a phrase the Highland was to use with good effect. A through carriage was put on between London (King's Cross) and Strathpeffer, Whitelaw explaining that the company's aim was 'to bring to Strathpeffer a large number of those people who foolishly have in the past crossed the channel and gone to foreign countries to seek cures which can be worked just as well very much nearer home'. In the following year Euston became the London starting point of the Strathpeffer through coach. Also in 1909 Whitelaw announced that the company would build a prestige hotel of its own in Strathpeffer. It was opened in 1911.

Year in, year out the Highland Railway lavished attention on Strathpeffer. Few readers of the London dailies and the glossier weeklies and the main provincial papers could have been left in doubt that Strathpeffer existed and that it was to be reached by The Picturesque Line of The Empire. In far Bombay readers of *Times of India* were exhorted to head for Strathpeffer on their next home leave.

The Strathpeffer advertisements were as eye-catching as

they were ubiquitous. In one popular advertisement, *The Doctor Prescribes*, a prosperous-looking physician sat in his consulting room wagging an admonitory finger at the reader. 'Sick? Nonsense man! You are city sick, that's all. Go to the Highlands and take your golf clubs with you.' The doctor was at pains to tell his patient to be sure to book via Perth and Dunkeld. A variation of the doctor theme was boldly headed 'Everard Mathews MD to Jack Arbuthnot KC' and the text had the medical man saying, 'You're to come with us to Strathpeffer Spa and take the famous medicinal cures.' A more academic approach was made to readers of *The Lancet* and *British Medical Journal*. Practitioners were advised to consult *A Medical Guide to Strathpeffer* (64 pages bound in green leatherette obtainable free from the Highland Railway) for a complete description of the baths, waters and treatments available.

From time to time the doctor gave way to other colourful exponents of Strathpeffer's charms. *The Minister Muses* showed a man of the cloth sitting in his study in sombre mood 'longing for a sight of Strathpeffer.' *The Angler Advises* spoke of rivers brimful of fish asking to be caught, and *The Caddie Converses* dwelt on that functionary's life on the most magnificent of golf courses.

Certain newspapers published what ostensibly were weekly reports on the goings-on at the fashionable resorts but which in fact were paid advertisements. The following Highland Railway-inspired piece appeared in the *Daily Telegraph*:

> Fine weather continues.
> This week the special express has brought a large number of visitors to this Highland Spa and many English people, including retired military men and their families, are taking the cure.
> To the officers of the fleet now in the Firth the golf course proves a great attraction.
> Rivers are getting low for fishing but lochs afford good baskets.
> The day excursions to places of interest are popular.
> There are large encampments of Yeomanry in the district.
> The Highland Hotel. The best hotel in the Spa. Beside the Baths, the Wells and the Gardens. Inclusive terms till 14 July 10s per day.

CHAPTER 5

Saga of the Mixed Train

AN OBNOXIOUS RULE

At the monthly meeting of Inverness Town Council held in May 1891 there occurred a heated discussion on the subject of the mixed train. The present day reader may well wonder why douce local politicians should have bothered to discuss let alone become excited about the mixed train. Well, the mixed train was a way of life in the Highlands. In an area of thin time-tables the passenger carriage attached to the goods train was a blessing to many a traveller. As Bailie McKenzie pointed out: 'Carriages have been attached to nearly all the goods trains upon the Highland Railway for many years and no accident has ever occurred (*been reported* would have been a fairer choice of verb) in connection with them. They have proved a source of great convenience to the travelling public.' The reason for the excitement in the council chamber was that under the Regulation of Railways Act of 1889 the Board of Trade had served on the Highland Railway an edict which if carried out would all but eliminate the much-loved mixed train.

The mixed train was specially suited to the economy of the Skye line. On many days of the year there was insufficient traffic to justify the running of both a passenger and freight service so it made good sense to combine passenger and goods vehicles in one train. In the first 10 years of its existence all trains, except specials, on the Skye line had been classed as mixed. As the mixed train ambled across the country stopping at every station the engine shunted each station yard picking up and depositing wagons. On the outward journey from Dingwall the engine normally shunted the wagons for the next eastbound train and

93

placed them in a siding ready to be picked up. This procedure was observed except at Garve and Achnasheen where the eastbound engine did its own shunting. All this took time. Passengers had ample opportunity to exchange gossip with the station staff or even to repair to the nearest place within the meaning of the act for a dram.

With its mixed trains the Highland marshalled the goods vehicles behind the engine and the passenger coaches in the rear. This procedure was frowned upon by authority. Since the goods wagons did not have continuous brakes operated from the engine the continuous brakes on the carriages were isolated and inoperable. While the train was in motion the only brakes available were those on the engine and the hand brake in the rear van. If a coupling between wagons broke on a rising gradient only the guard's handbrake was available to stop the severed rear portion. A circular, 'breaking asunder on inclines', mentioned in chapter 2, told the driver how to recover his broken off train safely on a falling gradient. There was no corresponding circular telling him what to do if a coupling broke on a rising gradient and his passenger carriages disappeared back down the line. When a mixed train stopped at a station the passenger carriages were left standing on the line while shunting was carried out with the goods wagons.

The new Act called for a radical reduction in the number of mixed trains run on any railway. It also made it compulsory for passenger vehicles to be marshalled next to the engine with the goods wagons in the rear. The passenger carriages had to be fitted with continuous brakes. This meant that the driver had control of the brake on every wheel of the passenger stock. In the event of a breakaway the pipe of the continuous brake would sever and the brakes would be applied on all carriage wheels automatically. In practice a driver would have to deposit his passenger carriages securely in a siding before commencing shunting operations and attach them to the rest of the train at the end of every shunt – a time-consuming process. Indeed, at many Highland wayside stations the layout was such that the manoeuvre would have been impossible without heavy expenditure in new track work. It was small wonder that

Highland opinion was disturbed. Inverness Town Council urged the Highland Railway to protest about 'this obnoxious rule' to the Board of Trade. Local organisations including Easter Ross Farmers' Club sent memorials to London petitioning for the preservation of the mixed train.

The Callander & Oban, too, was handicapped by the Act. Protest meetings took place at Oban and the Argyll County Council petitioned the Board of Trade. Andrew Dougall and John Anderson were as one in their fight for the mixed train. The Board of Trade was unmoved. Anderson accepted reluctantly the Westminster *dictat*. The *Railway Times* reported that the C & O 'has had to cancel a large number of local trains.' Dougall stood firm.

An order had been served on the Highland Railway on 16 February 1891 requiring the company to be in a position to comply fully with the terms of the Regulation of Railways Act by 16 August 1893. The time lag of $2\frac{1}{2}$ years was designed to allow the company to fit all its passenger stock with continuous brakes and modify its stations so that they could handle mixed trains with passenger carriages marshalled next to the engine.

The Highland Railway had never felt itself bound to adhere slavishly to London-promulgated rules. The Highland had its own way of doing things and it was not always Westminster's way. For instance there was the Highland's special method of detaching pilot engines from double-headed trains. When a double headed train was about a mile from a station where the pilot engine was due to come off and was running at about 35 or 40mph the fireman of the train engine walked along the framing and uncoupled the pilot. The pilot driver then opened up and drew ahead of the train which followed at its usual speed. The pilot ran into the loop, the signalman reversed the points and the train passed through the platform road. All very neat and time-saving. The Highland got away with this until one morning in November 1902 the newly detached pilot of the 10.10am mail from Inverness to Perth got safely into the loop at Dalwhinnie only to find that the train was following along the ballast between the two tracks, having been derailed when the signalman failed to display his usual dexterity with the points.

It was not surprising that the Highland took the admonition from London lightly. Dougall dispatched a lofty letter to the Board of Trade stating that the Highland Railway Company had been operating mixed trains for years without accident (an arguable point) and the company continued to operate mixed trains as if the Board of Trade and Acts of Parliament never existed. But within a year the Skye line was the setting of a mixed train near-disaster that could not be ignored.

ACHNASHELLACH

Donald McLeod lived a lonely life. He was stationmaster at Achnashellach and he was all on his own at the little single platform station which had changed little in the 22 years of its existence. He had no staff. His nearest colleagues were at Achnasheen 11 miles to the east and Strathcarron $5\frac{1}{2}$ miles to the west. All around him were mountains and empty moors among which the thin strand of the railway lost itself a short distance from his lonely outpost. In summer Donald's working day began at 6am and ended at 8pm; in winter his hours were 8am to 8pm. He operated the signals and points, worked the telegraph, assisted with the shunting and cleaned the office as well as selling the occasional ticket and dealing with the meagre paper work which his situation demanded. He was (almost) the 'compleat railwayman'. Donald's day was punctuated by the arrival and departure of the three trains each way during summer and two in winter, at best six movements in 14 hours. A highlight in summer would be the arrival of important guests for the shooting lodge, but in winter passengers were few. The station siding with a capacity of six wagons was more than adequate for Achnashellach's requirements. More often than not it was used as an engineer's siding.

By the autumn of 1892 Donald McLeod had been 17 years at Achnashellach. On the evening of 14 October he sat in his little wooden office-cum-bed-sitter waiting to attend to the last train of the day, the 4.20pm mixed from Dingwall to Strome Ferry. It was due at 6.10pm, but it had been offered by Achnasheen

37min late so he did not expect it to arrive before 6.45pm. The railway approached Achnashellach from the east on a rising gradient of 1 in 60 over a distance of 1550yd then just before it reached the platform it dropped at 1 in 400 towards the station.

Donald heard the train in the quietness of the still night when it was still a long way off. Then came the familiar sound of the Skye bogie labouring up the incline. When he went out on the platform to receive it the night was dark and showery and the paraffin lamp on the wall of the office did little to relieve the gloom. The engine shut off just before it crested the ridge and the train stopped with the engine standing just short of the siding points. Some of the goods wagons were on the gradient falling through the station but most of the train including all the passenger carriages was over the crest and standing on the 1 in 60 falling towards Achnasheen.

The journey had not been uneventful so far. Alexander McDonald the driver had worked the morning train from Strome Ferry through to Inverness. He had left Inverness piloting the 3.15pm double-headed Wick train, and at Dingwall, where the train had divided, McDonald with Skye bogie No 74 had taken over the Strome Ferry portion.

When the train left Dingwall 22min late it consisted of 14 vehicles, the goods vehicles being marshalled behind the engine and the passenger carriages in the rear in accordance with Highland Railway custom, but not in accordance with Board of Trade rules. At Achnasheen a saloon was detached. Also at that station McDonald was informed that there were two passengers for Glencarron platform on the train.

During the stop at Glencarron Donald Fraser the guard applied his brake. It was a Newall brake, a hand-operated system where by using a wheel in the van the guard could activate a complicated mechanism of rods and mechanical couplings to apply the brakes in the two adjoining passenger carriages which were a third class and a first class, both four-wheeled. As Fraser released the brake the wheel came away in his hand. The pinion spindle had broken, rendering the brake ineffective on the two rear passenger coaches. Fraser went forward to the engine and discussed the situation with McLeod whereupon both men went to the van and inspected the brake. The driver decided it was safe to proceed. The train left Glencarron with four loaded wagons, two vans, one empty wagon, one loaded horse box, one composite carriage containing a second class passenger, one empty first class carriage, a third class carriage with eight passengers and a van. The only effective brakes were those on the engine and tender.

The business on hand when the train arrived at Achnashellach was the transference of the first two wagons, which were loaded with sleepers, into the siding. In a movement of this kind the engine was first detached and run along the main line clear of the siding points. The wagons were then tailroped into the siding by the train crew. With the shunt completed the engine set back on to its train ready for departure.

There was no rigid demarcation of duties on the Skye line. Everybody did a little bit of everybody else's job when occasion demanded. That night Donald McLeod went to operate the siding points, and the driver walked down one side of the train pinning down wagon brakes. Eventually he got to the composite carriage on which he applied the brake using the external side wheel provided for the purpose. McDonald presumed that Donald Fraser had applied the brakes on the other two passenger vehicles using a similar method. But the Newall system was still coupled up and the side wheel could not operate the brakes until the Newall mechanism was disengaged. That was a lengthy process difficult if not impossible to accomplish in the dark. Fraser did nothing about it. Nor did any of the train crew tell the stationmaster that the Newall brake was out of action.

Alexander McDonald walked back up the train and when he reached his engine he prepared to uncouple it. He got between the tender and the first wagon and called on Allan Tosh his fireman to ease the engine back to slacken the coupling. As the buffers clinked the driver lifted the coupling from the wagon. Almost at once the train began to move slowly away from him. McDonald immediately tried to replace the coupling, but the gap between engine and wagon was already too great. He called on Tosh to back up the engine but as more and more of the train got on to the 1 in 60 falling gradient its speed increased. McDonald, with the coupling poised ready to slip on the hook stumbled along in the gap between engine and train, an extremely dangerous position in the almost total darkness. Fraser, who had returned with the tailrope shouted to the driver to jump clear, which he did. The stationmaster and crew watched helplessly as the entire train vanished into the night.

There is no clear account of what happened next. Certainly *nothing* was done for eight minutes. No doubt the four men at Achnashellach, shocked by what had happened, argued among themselves about what action to take. They knew that the train with its passengers was gathering speed down the twisting, steeply-descending line. It was Donald McLeod who suggested that the engine be sent in search of it. Accordingly, with McDonald and Tosh on the footplate and Fraser standing on the engine steps No 74 set off tender first in the wake of the runaway train.

The night was pitch dark. The men on the engine peered ahead as the Skye bogie slipped cautiously down the slope, but nothing was to be seen. No 74 ran on for a mile. It had reached the bottom of the incline and had begun to climb on a 1 in 375 gradient when Fraser spotted the light of his van some distance ahead. From his viewpoint he could not tell how far off the light was or whether it was stationary or still moving. It was in fact moving back to Achnashellach. The runaway had climbed up 500yd of 1 in 375 and had had its momentum arrested on the succeeding stretch of 1 in 75. Then it had begun to move back.

The collision took place 200yd from the foot of the gradient. The leading wagon of sleepers crashed into No 74's tender and was derailed. The rest of the train kept to the rails and was undamaged. Eight of the nine passengers complained of minor bruising or shock. Fraser explained to them what had happened and led them on foot to Achnashellach where they joined a special train summoned by telegraph from Strome Ferry. It departed at 9.10pm.

On 2 December 1892 David Jones inscribed the following note in his black book:

> Alex McDonald, Engineman, is fined 20s for contributing to the acci-
> dent of 14 October at Achnashellach through his not taking precautions
> to prevent the separation of the train and using sufficient care and judge-
> ment afterwards when going in search of escaped portion.

The Board of Trade was displeased with the Highland over
Achnashellach and the department's inspecting officer
expressed his displeasure in the strongest terms. The Highland
assumed a posture of offended dignity. There followed a remarkable correspondence between the Highland Railway
Company and the Board of Trade in which the railway company insisted that the department's attitude to mixed trains
and their marshalling was wrong and the Highland attitude
was right. Following an animated board discussion on 8
December 1892. Andrew Dougall wrote as follows to Courteney
Boyle, Assistant Secretary, Board of Trade:

> I am instructed to point out that if the train on the occasion referred to
> had been marshalled in the manner set forth in the order served on the
> company dated 16 February 1891, and the carriages placed next the en-
> gine, there is little doubt that the passengers would have sustained very
> serious injury and probably a loss of life would have occurred.

Boyle referred the letter to Major Marindin who had conducted the official inquiry into the Achnashellach accident. He
replied on 15 December:

> On the contrary, if the carriages had been next to the engine they
> would not have run away at all because it would have been impossible to
> place the two wagons on the siding at Achnashellach unless the carriages
> had remained coupled on to the engine. This is entirely irrespective of the
> question of brakes; but speaking generally the running away of a mixed
> train in which the carriages are fitted with an automatic continuous
> brake is most improbable.

Dougall was not to be moved from his position. On 17
December he replied to Courteney Boyle.

> It is clear that under the order of February 1891 the passenger carriages
> would have been next the engine and remained in that position while the
> shunting at Achnashellach was performed. That being so it is obvious
> that when the engine backed in search of the train which had run down
> the incline the passenger carriages would first have come in contact with
> the train and would have, doubtless, smashed like the wagon of sleepers
> which Major Marindin describes in his report and as the passenger car-
> riages are less strong than the dumb-buffered wagon the damage to them
> would have been greater than actually took place.

Only 30 years separate these photographs. *Above:* the old order with Skye bogie
No 33, still in Highland livery, heading a goods train in 1926.
Below: an LMS Class 5 4–6–0, the standard class on the line from the 1930s
until the end of steam in the 1960s, shunts a goods at Strome Ferry in 1956.
D. H. Stuart; J. Templeton

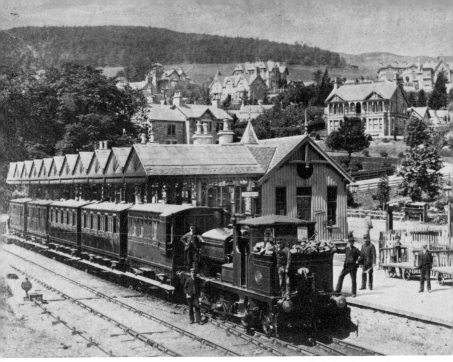

Above: Strathpeffer in its prime. No 13 *Strathpeffer*, an 0–4–4 saddle tank, was built specially for the branch by the Highland Railway. *J. Templeton collection*
Below: Strathpeffer in early LMS days with former Highland 'Yankee' 4–4–0 tank No 15014 at the head of a mixed train. *Locomotive & General Railway Photographs*

Courteney Boyle replied disdainfully:

> I am to acquaint you for the information of the directors that the Board of Trade cannot suppose that such an extraordinary procedure as that of sending back an engine with passengers attached in search of the runaway goods wagons could have been adopted and to add to that they find nothing in the correspondence to make it necessary for them to consider any modifications of the order made under the Regulation of Railways Act of 1889.

Dougall entered the fray again on 31 December:

> The siding at Achnashellach holds six wagons within the Scotch (sic) block, and when the train arrived there were three wagons already in it. The passenger portion of the train consisted of one first class, one third class and one large tri-composite and one brake van and under the Regulation of Railways Act 1889 these vehicles would have been next the engine, but the siding would not have held them, and therefore they would have remained attached while the engine went in search of the runaway good wagons. It is clear, therefore, that the result would have been disastrous as I have already stated, and the probability is that there would have been a very serious loss of life whereas as it was, owing to the carriages being at the tail of the train the passengers escaped with very light injuries.
>
> You state you find nothing in the correspondence to make it necessary to consider any modification of the order under the Regulation of Railways Act 1889. The directors of the company continue to entertain a strong opinion that the order you refer to is inexpedient and will be attended with danger to the public. They hope, therefore, it will be modified. This opinion is based on experience gained in the practical working of mixed trains for nearly 40 years during which time no passenger has lost his life or even been seriously injured when travelling in mixed trains whereas if the passenger carriages had been placed next the engine as directed by the new order, loss of life and serious injuries undoubtedly would have occurred in several cases.
>
> I am instructed to say that if the order is enforced as it stands it will practically put an end to the running of mixed trains on the Highland line and the accommodation now offered to the public in the Highlands will be seriously curtailed. The Highland line serves eight counties having a population of 468,976 and you can judge the effect which the new state of things will entail on that large population, but, of course, the Board of Trade must take responsibility.

Dougall was fighting not just for Achnashellach but for a principle. The Highland ran 113 mixed trains daily, about half the total number of trains in the timetable, and if the Board of Trade had its way most of them would be abolished.

In Whitehall they must have come to regard the appearance of
a letter with an Inverness postmark with trepidation. On receipt of the latest rebuke from the truculent gentleman in the
north Major Marindin set out to compile a lengthy memorandum. In it the major expressed the view that it was largely
by luck that the Highland's mixed train accidents had not produced fatalities and he went on to detail two accidents in which
luck had leaned heavily on the company's side. In one a passenger carriage had been thrown into the sea and its seven occu-
pants escaped drowning by virtue of the fact that the tide was
out at the time. In another mixed train accident a composite
carriage had somersaulted down a 20ft embankment leaving its
frame and wheels half way down the slope, the body landing in
a field roof uppermost. On Achnashellach Major Marindin
commented:

> There would have been no difficulty whatever in unloading the pass-
> enger carriages at the station and, giving the servants of the company
> credit for ordinary intelligence, this is what probably would have been
> done for we cannot believe that if the passenger carriages, still loaded,
> had remained attached to the engine the driver and guard of the train
> with the sanction of the stationmaster would have pushed it back down
> the incline in the dark to search for the runaway goods wagons.

Marindin signed the memorandum on 10 January 1893 and on
the following day Major General Hutchinson, chief of the inspectorate, countersigned it before it was dispatched to Inverness.

Dougall was furious. In his reply he recounted how a passenger injured in a Highland mixed train accident had sued the
company in the High Court for £5000, Major Marindin himself
appearing as a witness for the plaintiff. The jury found for the
company and the plaintiff got nothing. Dougall listed six mixed
train accidents in which no passengers had been injured because, he maintained, the wagons were next to the engine. One
had occurred on the Skye line when the 7.50am up train from
Strome Ferry to Dingwall was derailed at Strathpeffer (Achterneed) due to a failure of a spring on the locomotive. In its reply
the Board of Trade dismissed one of the accidents as trivial,
stated that Dougall's account of three others differed from that

given in the corresponding Board of Trade reports and another, a spectacular derailment, had never been reported to the Board.

On 24 January 1893 Andrew Dougall administered the *coup de grâce* direct to A.J. Mundella, President of the Board of Trade. Ending a long tirade he wrote:

> I need scarcely point out that in any view it is impossible to carry out the necessary changes upon our railway system and methods of working by 16th of August next when the order of 16 February 1891 comes into operation. The directors therefore venture to request that you will cancel the order so far as it relates to the marshalling of mixed trains or at all events to suspend it indefinitely.

Dougall's scarcely disguised threat to ignore the Act was considered at top level in Whitehall. Messrs Hutchinson, Marindin and Yorke, the three senior men of the railway inspectorate, signed the report that went to Mundella. It concluded:

> The final paragraph of the general manager's letter involves a question which will require very careful consideration when 16th August 1893 arrives, but we are at a loss to see why the time allowed to this company for complying with the terms of the order is not sufficient seeing that it amounts to 2½ years from the date of issue, and that is as much as has been granted to any company of any importance and considerably more than that granted to most.

Major Marindin ended his own report on Achnashellach on a note of optimism:

> It is satisfactory to know that very shortly when the order issued by the Board of Trade under the Regulation of Railways Act of 1889 regarding the use of continuous brakes comes fully into operation on this railway it will be obligatory to have an automatic continuous brake in operation upon all passenger vehicles of the mixed train so that a recurrence of an accident of this description will be well-nigh impossible.

Poor innocent Major Marindin! He should have known that on the Skye line nothing was impossible.

ACHTERNEED

Achnashellach notwithstanding, the Skye line remained host to the mixed train. In August 1893, the 16th came and went unnoticed as far as the Highland Railway was concerned. Official and public opinion in the Highlands was firmly on the side of the company. Local MPs, whatever their political colour resented the blanket legislation which had dealt so ruthlessly with the railway. Their view was that while the Act imposed little or no inconvenience on railways with *London* or *Great* in their names it was punitive as far as Highland passengers were concerned. They expressed their opinions regularly in Parliament and urged that the Highland Railway be excused from implementing the Act. But authority was unbending. In September 1893 Mundella for the Board of Trade said in reply to a question by Mr Beith MP:

> The Regulation of Railways Act of 1889 was passed by Parliament in the interests of public safety. It was clearly the intention of the Legislature that continuous automatic brakes be provided if not for every vehicle on trains carrying passengers, certainly in all those vehicles in which passengers are conveyed. This cannot be done under present arrangements if the goods wagons in a mixed train are placed in front of the passenger vehicles. Although the Board of Trade are willing to allow a limited number of mixed trains it is an invariable condition that on such trains passenger carriages must be placed in front so as to allow of their being provided with a continuous brake. The Highland Railway is one with very severe curves and steep gradients and on such a railway it is especially necessary that the travelling public and the servants of the company should have that protection that is afforded by the continuous brake. The absence of such protection has led to many accidents in various parts of the United Kingdom and to several accidents on the Highland Railway itself. Compliance with the order may involve the company in some expense but not to the extent referred to by the honourable member. I am unable to exempt the Highland company from an obligation which has been willingly accepted by all the principal railway companies of the United Kingdom and by so doing allow them to endanger the safety of their servants and the travelling public.

The best the well-wishing MPs could extract from Parliament was a series of extensions of the date by which the conditions of the order had to be met. The final extended period expired on 1 January 1896.

Five years after Achnashellach mixed trains still trundled along the Skye railway. If the furore in press and Parliament caused a flurry in the Highland board room it is not reflected in the company minute books. A few laconic entries tell the story.

For instance, on 3 August 1897 the secretary recorded:

> The general manager reported that he had received a communication from the Board of Trade in reference to the running of mixed trains on the Dingwall & Skye line attention being called to the manner in which the vehicles are marshalled in the trains and desiring the observations of the directors on the subject. It was decided that a reply be given pointing out under what authority the mixed trains were run and that the reason for the present method of marshalling also be given.

The mixed train saga continued with another entry on 1 September.

> Letter from the Board of Trade enclosing a complaint from Lt General Gloag RE was submitted in which it was complained that mixed trains were being run upon the Highland line and that passenger carriages were being marshalled in the rear of goods wagons. Resolved that a reply be given that mixed trains were running with the sanction of the Board of Trade. The reason for the marshalling of the trains is also at present being stated.

The Board of Trade served on the Highland an ultimatum to implement the Act or face dire consequences. The company could stall no longer. On 20 September 1897 Dougall informed the Board of Trade that henceforward mixed trains would be run in accordance with the department's requirements. But on 5 October the following entry was made in the minute book:

> The general manager reported four accidents as having occurred during the month, one in connection with the working of the 6.15pm train from Dingwall to Strome Ferry on 25 September when a mixed train broke in two and the goods wagons and the passenger vehicles ran back to Dingwall and was stopped without injury to any person. This accident has been reported to the Board of Trade.

The accident which the secretary recorded so glibly (but condescended to report to the Board of Trade) was hair raising in the extreme and on a railway less blessed with luck would have ended in disaster.

The train involved was again the evening mixed train from Dingwall to Strome Ferry, now retimed to leave at 6.15pm. The engine was Skye bogie No 88 and the load behind the tender was very similar to that of the train at Achnashellach of five years before. There were nine good wagons, four passenger carriages a luggage van and a brake van. The goods wagons were marshalled next to the engine and there were no continuous brakes on the passenger carriages.

The train took six minutes to run down to Fodderty Junction and another eight minutes to climb to Achterneed, which was about normal. The load of 160 tons was heavy, but comfortably within the limit for the locomotive. It was when No 88 left Achterneed and got its teeth into the two mile climb at 1 in 50 to Raven Rock summit that the crew ran into trouble. The night was wet and stormy and the rails were greasy. The engine several times lost its grip and the driving wheels spun uselessly. Speed fell almost to walking pace. The Skye bogie struggled on up the slope in a flurry of steam and noise. Slipping was almost constant. Then when the train was $\frac{1}{4}$ mile short of the summit a coupling with a hidden fault broke under the strain of the rugging and tugging. The engine was left with five wagons. The rest of the train including all the passenger section began to run back down the incline.

The guard in his van at the rear thought the driver was setting back to Achterneed to divide his train. It was only when the speed reached about 10mph that he realised all was not well. The 90 tons of rolling stock gaining in speed passed through Achterneed station and lurching through a series of 20-chain reverse curves rattled on towards Fodderty Junction. The runaway swept round the long reverse curve leading to the junction, clattered over the points and ran on towards Dingwall. It lost some of its impetus on the gently rising gradient but had sufficient momentum left to smash through and demolish the level crossing gates at the Invergordon Road before coming to rest 200yds short of the junction with the north line at Dingwall.

Five days after the Achterneed affair the principal officers of the Highland Railway gathered at Aberfeldy in connection with the inspection of the branch line to that town. Dougall afterwards said that in the course of the day he was 'instructed verbally' to marshal mixed trains according to the Act as from the following day. On 27 October 'it was reported that the number of mixed trains on the Highland company's line would be reduced from 1st November to the extent of 50 trains per day purely passenger and purely goods trains being substituted'.

CHAPTER 6

Pie in the Sky Lines

The Crofters' War was followed by the Crofters' Commission whose members toured the Highlands for more than a year investigating the problems which had stung a normally peace-loving population into open revolt. One of the main conclusions of the Commission, which published its report in 1884, was that the economic plight of the crofters was due in part to inadequate transport. The only two railheads on the west coast, Strome Ferry and Oban were deemed to be insufficient to meet the needs of the community. New railways were recommended.

One result of the atmosphere created by the report was the successful floating of the West Highland Railway. This line was to run from Glasgow via Loch Lomond, the Moor of Rannoch and Fort William to Roshven on Loch Ailort and serve a new much-needed fishing port about mid-way between Oban and Strome Ferry. The railway was to be the first lateral line built through the West Highlands. But the site chosen for the railhead was near an isolated mansion house, the home of a retired university professor. He successfully opposed the scheme and so deprived the islanders of a third rail-connected port. The West Highland Railway was cut back to Banavie on the Caledonian Canal. The line was of great importance in that it linked Glasgow and Edinburgh with Fort William, but it was of little use to the fishing community.

Meanwhile, promoters elsewhere were putting forward ideas. The Highland Railway was willing to back financially an extension of the Skye railway from Strome Ferry to Kyle of Lochalsh. The West Highland Railway was already thinking in terms of an extension from Banavie to the coast at Mallaig some 20 miles south of Kyle of Lochalsh. Two private companies planned to run railways up the valleys leading from the Skye line to the coast which were explored by Mitchell in 1864 and there were two proposed lines that would cross Sutherland from points on the north line to ports on the west coast.

The Government indicated that only one line of the six would be granted financial aid, and in 1890 a Commission was sent to examine and report on the various schemes. The railways on which they were called to judge were:

Strome Ferry-Kyle of Lochalsh
Banavie-Mallaig
Garve-Ullapool
Achnasheen-Aultbea
Lairg-Laxford
Culrain-Lochinver

The Commissioners were required to decide:

1 Which of the projected schemes is best calculated to promote the interests of the fishing and crofting population in the districts in question.
2 What amount of assistance would be required from public funds in each case to secure construction of the line.
3 Which of the schemes if any they would recommend to the Government to assist.

The project was in effect a competition, the one and only prize being money to be used in the construction of a railway.

The Commissioners spent a year 'perambulating the West Highlands' as one paper put it. Andrew Dougall was interviewed in June 1890. He confirmed that his company was willing to invest £120,000 in extending the Skye railway to Kyle of Lochalsh. He also made it clear that the Highland would vigorously oppose the spending of public money on the Mallaig line which Dougall saw as a very real threat to his own company's traffic to and from Skye. Throughout the proceedings the Highland made much of the fact that it always had had the interests of the crofters at heart. The investigator was not to know that in June 1887 when a firm of agricultural chemists at Stowmarket in Suffolk sent a gift of 40 tons of fertiliser to the crofters and asked the Highland to let the consignment pass free between Inverness and Strome Ferry the company demanded the usual rate for the traffic.

The Commissioners departed and many months passed without a report being issued. Not only the railway promoters but the ordinary people of the Highlands became impatient and angry. On 17 April 1891 Jackson, Financial Secretary to the Treasury, informed Dougall privately that the Government would give his company a grant of £45,000 for the Kyle of Lochalsh extension. That seemed to settle the matter; an official announcement would seal it. Then in June 1891 the Government appointed a new Commission 'to go into the whole questions of railways to the West Coast.' In fact, the Commission spent only a fortnight in the Highlands. Its objective apparently was to take a second look at some of the recommendations of their predecessors.

The Commissioners. Lt General Hutchinson, Admiral Sir George Nares, and Mr Henry Tennant, lately general manager of the North Eastern Railway, arrived in Inverness on 27 June accompanied by their secretary Mr Nicolle and met the Highland directors in the Caledonian Hotel that day. Nicolle asked Dougall on what terms his company would construct lines from Culrain to Lochinver and from Ullapool to Lochinver, schemes that were to cost £250,000 and £420,000. The question was significant. It presumed that the Garve-Ullapool line would be constructed and it showed the importance the Commission attached to Lochinver. The village adjoined a good anchorage conveniently sited half way between Skye and Cape Wrath. The Commission thought that Ullapool was unsuitable as a fishing port but excellent as a packet station. What they visualised was a train running from Garve (or Inverness) to Ullapool and there dropping passengers for the Stornoway steamer before continuing to Lochinver with fish vans and general traffic. But only a stranger who did not know the country would have suggested building a railway through a jumble of rock and ribbon lochs that lay between Ullapool and Lochinver – as the Commissioners found for themselves when they visited the site a few days later.

In the second week in August the gentlemen met in Arisaig to consider their verdict, but many months were to pass before their report was made public.

THE GARVE & ULLAPOOL RAILWAY

The Garve & Ullapool Railway was looked upon as a likely winner. It was the only one of the six projects to have an Act of Parliament when the Commission came to the Highlands. The line was the key to the shortest route to the coast and the fastest passage to Stornoway. It was backed by influential people.

The story of the Garve & Ullapool began in January 1889 with the parishioners of Lochbroom, Elphine and Assynt sending a memorial to the Highland Railway urging the construction of a railway from Garve on the Dingwall & Skye to Ullapool. The Highland was less than lukewarm about the proposal; they saw the proposed line not as a feeder to their own line but as a means of diverting traffic away from Strome Ferry. That short sea passage would be an attraction to many. Nevertheless, the petitioners were told that if they promoted and built such a railway the Highland would work it on reasonable terms. When Dr Macdonald MP intervened on behalf of the petitioners he was given a similar answer. John Fowler, whose estate at Braemore straddled the route of the proposed line urged the Highland to make a flying survey of the railway. Bowing to public pressure the company instructed Murdoch Paterson to make the survey which was undertaken in July 1889 at a cost of £80. That was as far as the Highland was prepared to go.

John Fowler had come a long way since he had antagonised the directors of the Dingwall & Skye and Highland railways two decades earlier. He was engineer-in-chief of the great Forth Bridge then nearing completion and was about to receive a baronetcy for his achievement. His southern commitments were too onerous to allow him to give much of his time to the Ullapool line but his son John A Fowler set about promoting the railway and looking for finance. They made such progress that by the summer of 1890 the Highland undertook to assist them in preparing a Bill and got as far as approving a 'Heads of Working Agreement' with the promoters.

The Garve & Ullapool Railway Act received the Royal Assent on 14 August 1890. The directors were named as Mary Jane, Lady Matheson of Achary and the Lews, Donald Matheson, Major Duncan Matheson, John Arthur Fowler and Major James Houston. Sir John Fowler was consulting engineer. That the project had secured the services of an engineer whose name at that particular moment (the Forth Bridge had been opened in March) was world famous was a propaganda point of the first order. The line as envisaged in the Act was to be $33\frac{1}{2}$ miles long. It left the Skye line just west of Garve and wound its way north-westward up the valley of the Blackwater by continuous but not unduly severe gradients to a summit of 900ft at Braemore. Then came a spectacular descent into the valley of the River Broom with the railway winding round clefts in the mountainside and all the time plunging towards sea level at the head of Loch Broom. The final stretch took it along the north shore of Loch Broom to a terminus near the steamboat pier at Ullapool at the junction of Quay Street and Shore Street. Along the whole length of the route there was scarcely a house to be seen. The promoters gave the population as 30 persons per mile, almost certainly an over-estimate. The railway was to cost £240,000 and take five years to build.

The Ullapool promoters were to find that nothing in Wester Ross had changed since the days when the Dingwall & Skye directors argued and cajoled their way across the county. Alexander George Pirrie, a landowner on the route, booked his private station almost as soon as the course of the railway was known and employed Benjamin Hall Blyth an eminent Edinburgh engineer to see that his demands were properly recorded in the Act:

> The company shall not construct any public station on any part of the said estate but they shall construct on some part of the estate in such position as may be reasonably required by the said Benjamin Hall Blyth a platform on the railway and siding therefrom for the exclusive use and

accommodation of the owner at which no train shall be stopped other than with the consent of the owner and if and when reasonably required for the purpose of the estate any train shall be stopped at the said platform by signal.

Thus Mr Pirrie demonstrated in the year 1890 that a man with power, money and influence could by Act of Parliament stop any train on a public railway to suit his own purpose.

A start could not be made until a Government grant had been paid or at least promised. The promoters and their supporters became increasingly irritated over the lethargy of the Commission and the consequent delay in the announcement of Westminster's decision. On top of that the Highland's interest in the scheme was seen to be waning, perhaps not surprisingly since the company was convinced that its own scheme to extend to Kyle would be the only one chosen. Certainly the parent company made no moves to pursue the interests of the Garve & Ullapool with the London legislature. That was the position when in April 1891 there came a dramatic turn of events.

Throughout their histories the Highland and Great North of Scotland railways had been at loggerheads. The GNS had never forgiven the Highland for having stopped the GNS advance to Inverness half way across the country, and the linchpin of GNS policy ever since had been to take Inverness either by direct assault with a new line of its own or by obtaining running powers over the Highland. As recently as February 1891 the GNS had assured the Provost of Wick, who was promoting a line from Wick to Lybster and wanted the GNS to work it, 'The company is very anxious to get a footing in the Northern District.' All such attempts to date had failed.

Towards the end of April William Ferguson, chairman of the GNS, and Moffat, the company secretary, on the one hand, and John Arthur Fowler and Major Houston of the Garve & Ullapool on the other made their separate ways to London. They met on 23 April when Fowler disclosed that the Garve & Ullapool had severed relations with the Highland and that neither they nor the Government would be negotiating with that company in future. Fowler wanted the GNS to take over the working of the Ullapool line.

Here was the opportunity for which the GNS men had been waiting. With the Garve & Ullapool in its grasp they would be in a position to claim running powers over the Highland line all the way from Elgin to Garve a distance of $66\frac{1}{2}$ miles. Another possibility discussed that day was that the Garve & Ullapool might build an independent line from Garve to meet the north line at Muir of Ord, running powers being claimed from Elgin to the junction. During the course of the day Moffat called on Jackson, Secretary to the Treasury, and urged him to use his influence to obtain running powers for the GNS from Elgin to Muir of Ord or Garve. Jackson replied that only Parliament could dispense running powers.

The GNS men returned immediately to Aberdeen where a special meeting of the board took place on 25 April. Unfortunately Moffat could not be present through illness and a final decision was not taken until a resumed meeting on 29 April. The proposal was that the company would work the Garve & Ullapool in accordance with the agreement formally reached with Fowler and Houston in London. A director, Mr Edmond, moved an amendment 'that the board accept the proposal conditionally on Parliament giving running powers to connect with the Great North system and that if the promoters cannot admit the foregoing condition the board with much regret must decline the proposal.' So cocksure were the other directors of securing running powers that Mr Edmond's precautionary amendment was defeated by seven votes to three.

If the GNS had hoped to keep their deliberations secret they were to be disappointed. Jackson of the Treasury was less neutral than would have been expected of a Civil Servant. No sooner had Moffat of the GNS left his office on 23 April than Jackson wrote to the Highland informing the company that 'certain proposals' had been made to him by the GNS. On the following day Lord Colville, a director of the Highland who was in London at the time, dispatched to Inverness a full account of the GNS approach. Andrew Dougall left for London bent on arranging with Jackson 'for the protection of this company's interests.'

Later in the summer the matter was taken a stage further when the GNS agreed to take over the Garve & Ullapool lock stock and barrel and work the line as an isolated GNS branch. A Bill was drafted in which the Garve & Ullapool promoters sought to transfer their undertaking to the GNS. The Highland 'resolved to give such a Bill the determined opposition of this company.' The thought of GNS trains running along the Skye line creaming off already sparse traffic was one the Highland could not contemplate with equanimity. In the Bill the Ullapool promoters alluded to possible Government support. This infuriated Jackson who demanded that all references to the Treasury and possible Government aid be deleted.

The Bill was in Parliament when the long-awaited report of the West Coast Commission was published. 'The report of the special committee appointed to inquire into the various schemes for the railway development of the west coast of Scotland is not a very hopeful document,' commented the *Railway Times*. Indeed it wasn't. 'None of the suggested railway projects,' said the report, 'can be regarded as possessing a commercial basis or the elements of success as ordinary undertakings.' The reporters saw in the western section of the Ullapool line 'serious obstacles which would make construction costly and would involve very steep gradients.' The only positive result of the Commission's work was that, as anticipated, £45,000 was earmarked as a subsidy for the extension of the Skye line to Kyle of Lochalsh. There was a promise of favourable consideration for the Mallaig extension at a future date.

The report provoked anger in the Highlands. The newspapers told of hundreds of people from the Loch Broom area gathering in Ullapool and condemning the report as 'stupid, irritating and mischievous.' Commissions composed of Englishmen came in for harsh criticism. Mr P Campbell Ross of Ullapool, one of the most active supporters of the railway and himself a former officer of an English company wrote, 'As regards Royal Commissions and Departmental Committees, Highlanders mistrust them thoroughly as being composed of men who they think come north with their minds made up on a certain course and to enjoy a pleasant holiday at the expense of the country'. The Highland Railway was seen as the villain of the piece with Dougall as the arch traitor. 'Surely,' wrote Mr Ross sarcastically, 'such an astonishingly able manager as Mr Dougall could afford to be more liberal to bantlings he encouraged into the status of Parliamentary sanction as was the case with the Garve & Ullapool scheme which will yet be fought for by influential railways but I trust not won by the Highland'.

Undaunted, the promoters and their followers, backed by the GNS, continued their efforts to build the railway without Government help. Ross thought that a railway from Ullapool to Garve would be at least as important as the LNWR's line from Liverpool to London. Writing in the *Railway Times* he said, 'I do not suppose any one would venture to say that in the interest of the country at large the Mersey traffic to London would be more valuable to the public than the enormous supply of fresh fish now unused would be were there sufficient railway facilities for its thorough development'. The transfer Bill passed standing orders and was given a second reading in the House of Commons, the GNS agreeing to pay expenses up to £500 if the Bill went to Committee. But as the year progressed it became all too clear that without public money there was no hope of raising the requisite £240,000. The GNS began to get cold feet. At a special meeting of the board on 4 November 1892 it was agreed to continue with the sponsorship of the Bill only if the Government was willing to pay 3 per cent on the capital, allow the GNS 65 per cent of the gross revenue and concede the vital running powers over the Highland. These were impossible terms. But hope lingered on in Ullapool. When John Leng, the Dundee newspaper proprietor, was on holiday in the village in 1893 the villagers prevailed on him to run a campaign to secure the railway, which he did but to no avail. The last straw was the passing on 29 June 1893 of the Act allowing the Highland to make the extension to Kyle. A few days later the Ullapool promoters abandoned their scheme. The *Garve & Ullapool Railway (Abandonment) Act* was passed on 24 August.

One scene in the drama remained to be played. The Highland Railway sued in the Court of Session Mary Jane, Lady Matheson, and other promoters of the Garve & Ullapool for

£668 that being the cost to the Highland of promoting the Garve & Ullapool Bill. The Highland lost the case.

The Loch Maree & Aultbea Railway, a rival of the Ullapool scheme, never really got off the ground. It was to start at Achnasheen and run by the south shore of Loch Maree, Gairloch, and Poolewe to Aultbea on Loch Ewe a distance of 35 miles. The country traversed was as difficult as it was magnificent. The route was surveyed by Meek & Company of London and a Bill, vigorously opposed by the Highland, was presented in Parliament in 1893. The preamble was not proved.

LIGHT RAILWAY MANIA

In 1894 the West Highland Railway got its Act to make the extension to Mallaig. The Government proposed to give the company £45,000 to contruct a harbour and guaranteed a dividend of 3 per cent on the £260,000 required for the building of the line – terms very like those which had been sought by the Garve & Ullapool. The proposal provoked a nationwide political storm, the issue being whether public money should be given to a private company. It was not until 1896 that the *West Highland Railway (Guarantee) Act* was passed and the grant for the extension was authorised.

Also in 1896 there was passed the Light Railways Act which was intended to introduce a new era in rural railway history. Promoters were to be encouraged to build cheap lines capable of carrying light loads at low speeds in districts where the traffic would not justify the construction of a standard line. The new legislation resulted in a spate of railway schemes, some of them light railway revivals of recently rejected projects. In September 1898 when the Light Railway Commissioner visited Scotland he had in his files 35 applications for light railways.

John Arthur Fowler revived the Garve & Ullapool as a light railway and sought Highland support. Charles Steel from the North Eastern Railway who recently had taken the place of Dougall, who had retired, went to Braemore to see Fowler. He made it abundantly clear to him that on no account would the Highland put money into his company, but he offered to work

Above: The Kyle-Kyleakin 'car' ferry in 1905 with a gipsy caravan propped precariously athwart the vessel. Cars were specially insured for the crossing. *Graham E. Langmuir*
Below: Car ferries at Kyleakin in 1936. *John Thomas*

Top: Far from home. Ex-Devon Belle observation car on the turntable at Kyle. A circle for the turntable had to be scooped out of the solid rock. *J. Templeton*
Above: An excursion train passing along the shore of Loch Carron in 1906. The engine is a Small Ben and the second and third vehicles are excursion saloons introduced that year with the Skye line specially in mind. *J. Templeton collection*
Below: The Skye line in more recent years, with a British Railways class 27 diesel locomotive turning away from the sea, with Skye in the background to run alongside Loch Carron, soon after leaving Kyle of Lochalsh. *Derek Cross*

the line on the 1892 terms provided Fowler raised the necessary capital to build it. Nothing happened. An attempt to float the Loch Maree & Aultbea Railway as a light railway likewise failed.

In October 1896 a deputation from the 1st District Committee of Inverness County Council waited on Steel and inquired what the attitude of the Highland would be to a light railway in Skye. The Highland, in fact, had no desire to expend money on new railways west of Inverness, but it would not have been politically expedient for Steel to have come out in the open with a declaration of his company's attitude. Lip service had to be paid to the local authority. At that moment the railway fortress of Inverness was under siege. Not only was yet another GNS assault threatened from the east but the West Highland, backed by the North British, was striving to get into Inverness via Fort Augustus and the Great Glen. The proposed railway in Skye of which the councillors had got wind was to terminate not at Kyleakin but at Isleornsay which was within easy reach of the now authorised West Highland terminal at Mallaig. This was a situation fraught with danger for the Highland. Steel told the deputation that if the line was made to standard gauge and taken to Kyleakin instead of to Isleoronsay he would recommend to his board the provision of a steam ferry capable of conveying railway trucks between Kyleakin and Kyle of Lochalsh. His visitors stated themselves 'highly satisfied with what was stated to them.'

A week after the interview Messrs Anderson and Shaw who were Clerks and Treasurers to Inverness County Council inquired of the Highland how much money it was prepared to invest in railways in Skye. In an evasive reply Steel said that he had no idea of the cost of such lines but that he would make his own survey and reply in due course to the County Council. On 3 March 1897 he announced that a survey had been made of a short line running from Kyleakin across the island through Broadford to Torrin on Loch Slapin, but he gave no figures and no action was taken. In April when the local Member of Parliament put pressure on the Highland to give a decision Steel went over the ground again with the promoters. He reported to his board that he 'could not recommend a definite attitude.' Only the threat of competition could spur the Highland into action, and that competition soon was forthcoming.

The Hebridean Light Railway was the longest and most ambitious scheme proposed under the Light Railways Act. It envisaged 97 miles of railways in Lewis and Skye. In Skye the railway was to run the whole length of the island taking in all the principal places *except* Kyleakin. Branches from Dunvegan and Uig in the north were to converge just north of Portree before continuing south through Sligachan and Broadford to Isleornsay on the Sound of Sleat 10 miles distant from Mallaig. All its traffic was to be delivered to the West Highland at Mallaig and the railway itself like the West Highland would have been worked by the North British. Fortunately for the Highland the Hebridean Light Railway, although it attracted much publicity, turned out to be a maverick scheme thought up in London by people who knew little about Skye except its shape on a map.

Further attempts to induce the Highland to support light railways in Skye failed. When in March 1898 the District Committee of the Inverness County Council invited the Highland to build a line from Portree to Dunvegan with a branch to Uig the company refused. In June 1899 a Mr Barrington writing from Limerick sought the help of the local Member of Parliament Mr Baillie in enticing the Highland to build a $25\frac{1}{2}$-mile railway from Portree to Dunvegan for 60 per cent of the gross receipts diminishing to 50 per cent when revenue reached £9 per mile per week. The Highland refused to be tempted.

The 1890s saw the departure from the scene of four main characters who had witnessed the birth of the Skye line. In 1895 Andrew Dougall general manager and secretary retired having given 40 years of service to railways in the Highlands. There was a touch of sadness in the manner of his going. For many years he had taken decisions on his own that in other companies would have been matters for the full board of directors. He was given a free hand to the extent of raising stock worth many thousands of pounds, telling the directors about it afterwards. 'All financial agreements were left very much in my hands to carry out on behalf of the board as I thought best for the company,' he was to say. In the early 1890s Dougall allocated £150,000 of preference stock to himself and friends following which he adjusted the dividend terms causing the stock to appreciate whereupon he sold his holding at a profit of £21,000 to himself. Dougall claimed that the sum represented 'risk' money. The directors thought otherwise and he had to go.

In 1896 David Jones, whose ill-health had resulted in a deterioration in the locomotive department he had tended meticulously for 27 of the 41 years he had served the Highland, surrendered his office to Peter Drummond of the Caledonian Railway. In 1898 two stalwarts of the Skye line died – Murdoch Paterson, who had risen to be engineer-in-chief of the Highland, and Sir John Fowler who, old animosities forgotten, had been appointed consulting engineer to the company.

Highland Railway Tours for 1896.

Tickets available for two Calendar Months, with liberty to break the journey
at any point where Train or Steamer calls on the Route.

N.B.—The Routes may be reversed.

No. 1.—Inverness by Rail to **Dingwall** and **Achnasheen**, by Coach to **Loch-Maree** and **Gairloch**, by Steamer to **Portree (Skye)** and **Strome Ferry**, thence by Rail to **Inverness**. 1st or 3rd Class by Rail according to ticket, outside of Coach, and Cabin or Steerage of Steamer. Fare—1st Class, 38s ; 3rd Class, 24s 8d.

No. 2.—Inverness by Rail to **Dingwall, Achnasheen,** and **Strome Ferry**, Mr MacBrayne's Steamer to **Portree (Skye), Oban, Loch-Ness, Fall of Foyers,** and **Inverness.** Fare—1st Class Rail and Cabin Steamer, 49s 6d ; 3rd Class, 32s 4d. Also from Aberdeen, 84s 4d and 50s 5d.

No. 3.—Inverness by Rail to **Dingwall** and **Achnasheen** by Coach to **Loch-Maree** and **Gairloch**, Mr MacBrayne's Steamer to **Portree (Skye)**, |**Oban, Loch-Ness,** and **Inverness.** Fare—1st Class Rail, outside Coach, and Cabin Steamer, 53s 6d ; 3rd Class, 38s 4d. Also from Aberdeen, 88s 4d and 54s 11d.

No. 4.—Achterneed by Rail to **Strome Ferry**, Mr MacBrayne's Steamer to **Portree** and **Gairloch**, by Coach to **Loch-Maree** and **Achnasheen**, thence by Rail to **Achterneed**; or the route from Achnasheen may be reversed. Fare—1st Class Rail, outside Coach, and Cabin Steamer, 31s.

None of the Tourist Fares *via* Loch-Maree include Coachman's Fee between Achnasheen and Gairloch, which is 1s 6d for one Passenger and 2s 6d for a party of two.

No. 5.—Inverness by Steamer to **Fort-William** and **Oban**, thence by Rail to **Dalmally, Dunblane, Perth,** and **Dunkeld** to **Inverness.** Fare—1st Class, 58s ; 3rd Class, 30s 6d.

No. 6.—Inverness by Rail to **Killiecrankie, Dunkeld, Stirling, Edinburgh (Waverley),** and **Glasgow (N.B.),** Mr MacBrayne's Steamer to **Oban, Fort-William, Fall of Foyers,** and **Inverness.** Fares—1st Class Rail and Cabin Steamer, 65s 6d ; 3rd Class and Steerage, 33s 5d.

No. 7.—Inverness by Rail to **Killiecrankie, Dunkeld, Stirling,** and **Glasgow (Cal.),** Mr MacBrayne's Steamer to **Oban, Fort-William, Fall of Foyers,** and **Inverness.** Fare—1st Class Rail and Cabin Steamer, 61s 9d ; 3rd Class, 32s 3d.

No. 8.—Inverness by Rail to **Dingwall** and **Garve**, by Coach to **Lochbroom** and **Ullapool,** Mr MacBrayne's Steamer to **Stornoway, Portree,** and **Strome Ferry,** thence by Rail to **Inverness.** Fare—1st Class, 32s 6d. To holders of Tickets for this Tour, the Fare by Coach from Garve to Ullapool, payable to the Coachman, will be 7s 6d, which includes his fee.

No. 8a.—Inverness by Rail to **Dingwall** and **Strome Ferry,** Mr MacBrayne's Steamer to **Portree (Skye),** by Coach to **Dunvegan,** Mr MacBrayne's Steamer to **Lochmaddy (North Uist), Rodel, Tarbert (Harris), Portree,** and **Strome Ferry,** thence by Rail to **Achnasheen** and **Inverness.** Fares—1st Class, 44s 7d ; 3rd Class, 25s 3d.

No. 8b.—Inverness by Rail to **Dingwall** and **Achnasheen,** by Coach to **Loch-Maree** and **Gairloch,** Mr MacBrayne's Steamer to **Portree (Skye),** by Coach to **Dunvegan,** Mr MacBrayne's Steamer to **Lochmaddy, Rodel, Tarbert (Harris), Portree,** and **Strome Ferry,** thence by Rail to **Inverness.** Fares—1st Class, 48s 6d ; 3rd Class, 32s. For other Tours see H. R. Coy's Tourist Programme.

Although the stations along the line attracted few resident tourists (Strathpeffer excepted) the railway was vital to tourists in transit. This extract from Cornet's timetables of 1896 shows that the line was a key link in seven out of ten tours offered by the Highland Railway.

CHAPTER 7

Through to Kyle

EXTENSION

When construction of the extension from Strome Ferry to Kyle of Lochalsh began, the *Railway Times* commented:

> It will be a remarkable piece of railway on account of the difficulties of construction. Throughout the entire length it will have to be carried through rock which is of a character very difficult to work while the stations necessary will practically have to be excavated. It will undoubtedly prove one of the most picturesque pieces of railway ever constructed in Scotland.

Contracts were let in September 1893 to John Best. The railway was to cost £83,873, the piers at Kyle of Lochalsh £37,099 and land, stations and buildings £150,000. It was the most costly railway built in Britain up to that time. The government's contribution of £45,000 was hotly criticised in some circles. Labour was largely indigenous. Along the line of the railway by the shore of Loch Carron were about two hundred crofts and the crofters were recruited to work on the line. Compensation payments for land were paid to 170 of them.

It took Best four years to blast a roadbed through the gneiss and quartzite. At Kyle of Lochalsh 105,800 cubic yards of material were cut out of the virgin rock to make a place for the station and yard. A neat circle was scooped out of the rock to accommodate the turntable. Every foot of ground had to be fought for. Weather was a constant hazard. In 1894 almost no work was done during five months of heavy rain and work was further delayed by the aftermath of the great snowstorm of 1895 when the railway east of Strome was closed for a week. Slowly the spectacular railway with the new terminal village built to

125

service it took shape.

Best had hoped to have the line complete by late summer of 1897 and it would have been finished on time had it not been for the fact that at the last minute the crofters deserted the workings to harvest their crops. Many, sensing that their jobs on the railway would be short-lived, did not return but instead sought work on the Mallaig and Invergarry railways then just beginning. The contractor found himself with the last four miles of the line laid but without top ballast, and without men to lay the ballast. It was 2 November 1897 before the first train steamed into Kyle and stopped in the shadow of the mountains of Skye thus fulfilling the vision of the men who had met at Westminster more than 33 years before.

The rejoicing which greeted the arrival of the first train at Kyle was not shared by the disappointed Ullapool lobby who regarded the railway as the fruit of treachery. By a trick of fate P. Campbell Ross, formerly of Ullapool, found himself living beside the new railway on opening day. 'Let me now mention,' he informed readers of the *Railway Times*, 'that I am on the scene of what I may charitably call Dougall's Folly. He has left it as a legacy to his directors and his successor. As an engineering feat it does credit to Mr Paterson and his staff, and whatever his profit in connection with the undertaking may be, the contractor has done his work so well that I trust his next contract will be greatly more advantageous to his bank account. The whole thing was a blunder.'

The Highland Railway worked hard to create a thriving community on the bare rock at Kyle. People wanting to build houses were given sites at very low rates. A site for a library was provided at a nominal rent of 5s per annum and Highland Village Industries got a site on modest terms as did the proprietors of various shops. Kyle of Lochalsh began to look lived-in. Even property speculators tried to move in. An English gentleman offered £1000 and an annual rental of £5 for the station refreshment room. A compatriot, Dr. Ogilvie of Co Durham wanted to buy the small hotel the company had established at Kyle for conversion into a hydropathic 'for the treatment of invalids by electricity'. These overtures were

THE HIGHLAND RAILWAY COMPANY.

OPENING OF LINE

FROM

STROMEFERRY

TO

KYLE OF LOCHALSH

The above Section of the Highland Line, which gives access to some of the Grandest and most Picturesque Scenery in Scotland, will be

OPENED FOR TRAFFIC

On TUESDAY, the 2nd NOVEMBER, 1897.

By means of this Railway, direct access will be obtained to the Western Coast of Scotland, and greatly increased facilities given for reaching the Isle of Skye and the Western Isles.

The principal sea route for Steamers and other Vessels off the West Coast of Scotland is past the Pier at Kyle of Lochalsh. Arrangements for Steamers coaling, and for loading and discharging merchandise, and for passengers joining and leaving vessels, will be made.

The distance from the Pier at Kyle of Lochalsh to the Pier at Kyleakin in the Isle of Skye, is only half-a-mile, and a Steam Ferry Boat will ply between these two piers.

The Service of Trains will be as follows:—

	A.M.	A.M.	P.M.		A.M.	A.M.	P.M.
Kyle of L'chalsh dep.	6 0	10 30	4 55	Inverness ....dep.	8 35	10 50	5 10
Duirinish .... ,,	6 11	10 41	5 10	Dingwall.......... ,,	9 35	11 55	6 15
Plockton .... ,,	6 17	10 47	5 20	Stromeferry...... ,,	11 51	2 10	9 0
Stromeferry...... ,,	6 30	11 0	5 40	Plockton.......... ,,	12 3	2 22	9 17
Dingwall .... ,,	8 35	1 10	8 28	Duirinish......... ,,	12 8	2 28	9 24
Inverness.........ar.	9 32	2 5	9 25	Kyle of L'chalsh ar.	12 20	2 40	9 40

For Information as to Passenger Train Charges apply to W. GARROW, Superintendent of the Line; and for Goods Train Rates to GEO. THOMSON, Goods Manager.

CHARLES STEEL, General Manager.

Railway Offices, Inverness, November, 1897.

rejected. The Highland preferred to extend and develop the hotel which occupied a magnificent site looking out on the mountains of Skye. A Mr McCrae proposed to the board that the station be renamed 'Kyle' since nobody ever called it by any other name. But the board favoured retaining the sonorous Kyle of Lochalsh.

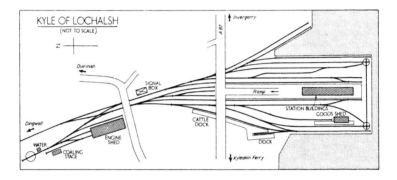

There were two stations on the extension – Plockton and Duirinish, Duncraig Halt being added at a later date between Strome Ferry and Plockton mainly for the use of the Mathesons of Duncraig Castle. Three trains were provided between Inverness and Kyle of Lochalsh in each direction daily except on Sundays. The passenger trains took between 3hr 32min and 3hr 50min to complete the journey while the mixed trains were allowed 4hr 30min. Two piers at Kyle were capable of servicing passenger and cargo vessels at all states of the tide. Handling facilities offered to shippers included office accommodation, fish tables, craneage and coaling berths. Strome pier was closed and abandoned. The Highland Railway also announced the abandonment of the lighthouses and markers it had placed in Loch Carron by order of the Northern Lights Commissioners but that body refused the railway company permission to abandon the lights. Not unreasonably the Highland took the view that since it had been compelled to provide the lights at its own expense and now that it no longer required them it should be allowed to abandon them or transfer the cost to those whom the lights would now benefit. After four years of wrangling the railway company was relieved of its obligation to maintain the lights.

The timetable was retained with minor variations until the opening of the Mallaig Extension on 1 April 1901. The steamers from that date began their voyages at Mallaig before sailing up to Kyle taking on passengers and freight at both ports. Travellers from Stornoway and Portree had the alternative of leaving the steamers at Kyle and travelling south via Inverness and Perth or continuing to Mallaig and using the North British trains which ran via Fort William and the West Highland Railway. The West Highland route was quicker and cheaper than the Highland route and traffic on the Skye railway noticeably dropped.

For some years there had been a public demand for an express train from Dingwall to the west coast in connection with the steamers, and it was the advent of the Mallaig Extension that induced the Highland to provide such a train in the summer timetable of 1901. It departed from Dingwall at 10.36am on the arrival of the train from the south and, stopping only at Garve, Achnasheen and Strathcarron, was in Kyle at 1.0pm. The regular train followed at 11.10am reaching Kyle at 2.15pm. There was no express in the up direction, but the 6.10am boat connection from Kyle was retimed to leave at 5.10am giving an 8.0am arrival at Dingwall and a connection to the south. The 11.25am mixed up train crossed four trains in the course of its journey – the 9.0am ex-Dingwall at Strome Ferry, the 10.36am express at Strathcarron, the 11.10am passenger at Achnasheen and a Strathpeffer branch train at Fodderty Junction. (There were ten trains each way on the branch.)

The Kyle of Lochalsh express was not a success. It ran to time, but because of the persistent late arrival of the steamer from Mallaig passengers were kept standing on Kyle pier for an hour or more. Not infrequently they were still waiting for the boat when the following stopping train arrived. The Skye line passengers were at the mercy of timekeeping on the West

Highland.Railway for the steamer could not leave Mallaig until the arrival of the train from Glasgow. Appeals to MacBrayne proved fruitless and the express was withdrawn in 1904 never to be restored. Over the years requests for a resumption of the service were received at Inverness. Correspondents received a stock letter saying that the Highland Railway would be pleased to restore the train on condition that MacBrayne guaranteed a speedy connection at Kyle.

In the winter of 1901 the service dropped to two trains a day each way. The down trains left Dingwall at 11.10am and 3.40pm reaching Kyle at 1.50pm and 7.10pm. The corresponding up services departed Kyle at 6.10am and 11.0am reaching Dingwall at 9.27am and 1.40pm. There were six trains each way on the Strathpeffer branch.

The West Highland continued to make inroads into Skye line traffic. William Whitelaw told the Highland shareholders: 'Some people in Edinburgh imagine that an unimportant line running up to Fort William and Mallaig is the only line in the Highlands and they never think of going elsewhere. That is a fact, and we of the Highland Company point out that the only line by which people can see the Highlands is the Highland line and we have secured some of the traffic'. Three months after making that speech Whitelaw was appointed a director of the North British while retaining the chairmanship of the Highland. Henceforward he was committed to serving both the *only line* and the *unimportant line* to the Highlands.

Keen competition for fish traffic persisted. In the herring season there would be canvassers from the North British, the Callander & Oban and the Highland in Stornoway, each fighting for a share of the traffic. William Whitelaw told of a day when three vessels sailed from Stornoway for Oban, Mallaig and Kyle and three special trains, each carrying a third of the catch left their respective ports for London. At Berwick all three trains were combined to form one train. Whitelaw described the process as 'monstrous waste.'

The overall pattern of travel did not change in the years leading to World War I. Basically the railway remained a through route to the islands with the intermediate stations attracting little traffic. Loch Maree and its magnificent surroundings had been isolated and costly to visit and a new excursion put the area within easy reach of the day traveller from Inverness. The route was by train from Inverness to Achnasheen thence by coach to destination. Very occasionally excursions involving short sea trips from Kyle were advertised. On one such occasion PS *Glencoe* carried train passengers from Kyle to Loch Duich and back.

The hotel on the up platform at Achnasheen was owned by the railway company but leased to private proprietors who were usually also responsible for the coaching and stabling arrangements for the Achnasheen-Loch Maree service. The hotel kept its own cows, which were accommodated in close proximity to the guests. There was an occasion when a visiting Medical Officer of Health disapproved of the arrangement with the result that the Highland Railway was required to spend £75 10s on a new byre, £13 8s on a concrete channel and gulley traps and £1 10s on alterations to the dung pit.

A spin along the Skye railway was still regarded as a bit of an adventure. One traveller who made the acquaintance of the line in 1909 considered he had taken his life in his hands in using it. He published his impressions in *The North Star*:

> From Attadale to Strome Ferry the line runs alongside the edge of the loch winding in and out under the shadow of a huge rocky hill which threatens to fall at many places and crush the train to matchwood or throw it into the deep blue waters of the loch. The run is one of thrills to the newcomer and to all travellers who realise that little would send all to eternity. That no accident has befallen a train in the past (to our knowledge) is no guarantee that the same happy result will be enjoyed in the future. That nothing has happened can be put down to the extreme care of the railway officials. Flags waved by men on the lineside here and there along the most dangerous parts assure the driver that all is well.

Strathpeffer continued to prosper. In 1910 the village had its best year ever with every hotel bed taken and potential visitors having to be turned away. It was in the following year that the company opened its own Highland Hotel. The village got its own prestige train, the *Strathpeffer Spa Express*, which on Tuesdays only left Aviemore at 2.30pm (after the arrival of the train from the south) and, avoiding Inverness station by the spur

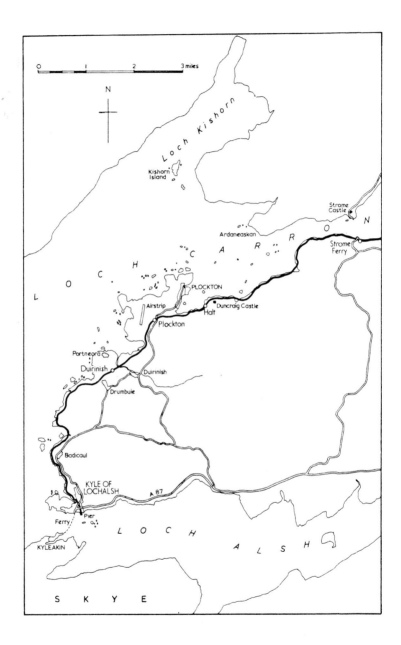

Map showing the meanderings of the line between Strome Ferry and Kyle of Lochalsh along the coast.

linking south and north lines and stopping only at Dingwall, reached Strathpeffer at 4.15pm. The train, composed of immaculately turned out bogie carriages and hauled by a Castle 4–6–0 or Loch 4–4–0 carrying a headboard, made an impressive sight.

At first the outbreak of war in August 1914 had little obvious effect on the Skye line. Strathpeffer now offered 'The Safest and Best Holiday.' Aberdonians in particular were urged to seek sanctuary in Strathpeffer the implication being that their city was under the threat of German invasion. The typical Strathpeffer advertisement of the period showed a young mother and her schoolboy son gazing wistfully from a carriage window and saying, 'Come with us'. Papa presumably was at the front and the family was bent on soothing away the strains of wartime in the waters of 'the Strath.'

The halcyon days were soon to end. The whole of the north of Scotland was surrounded by strategic waters. The area north of the Caledonian Canal was closed to all but service personnel, residents and approved visitors with permits. The *Strathpeffer Spa Express* ceased to run after the 1915 season and the Highland Hotel was taken over by the military. Although a normal passenger service was shown in the public timetables the trains could be cancelled to make way for naval traffic. Coach and steamer services in connection with the trains were abandoned or severely restricted. Traffic reached a peak in 1917–18 when the Americans operated a base at Kyle of Lochalsh. Many thousands of mines were landed at the piers and taken by rail to a depot near Invergordon. The Skye railway, forced to carry traffic for which it had not been designed, was severely taxed. The Admiralty put in new loops and improved signalling to increase line capacity.

The Highland Railway had neither the engines nor the staff to cope with the traffic generated by the war. Engines were borrowed from other railways and William Whitelaw appealed to local Boy Scouts to volunteer for railway tasks. On 1 March 1918 22 foreign engines were at work on the Highland system some of which appeared from time to time on the Skye line. NBR No 504 *Glen Cona* was at work on the line in 1917. In the winter of 1917 an unexpected visitor was CR No 53, one of the 4–6–0s built for the Callander & Oban Railway by J F McIntosh. Although these engines had worked on the Oban line for many years with conspicuous success Inverness was unwilling to risk No 53 on the Skye line.

It so happened that No 53 was standing at Dingwall one cold winter day when word was received that No 94 *Strath Tay* had failed on the climb from Garve to Raven's Rock. There wasn't a spare engine within miles so the decision was taken to send in No 53. The only fitter at Dingwall shed got aboard with his tools and the Caledonian engine took to the Skye line, the driver having been warned not to exceed a speed of 15mph. At Achterneed they took on No 94's fireman who had walked through the section with the tablet.

They found No 94 sitting on the bank with a train of American naval stores on her tail. It was believed that several cylinder rings had disintegrated. The fireman dropped part of the engine's fire on the ground beside the fitter to give him a modicum of comfort as he worked in the biting cold. At length the cylinder head and cover were removed and the broken rings taken out. The bits and pieces of No 94 were deposited on the front running plate and No 53 set off for Dingwall with the dead engine and train in tow. At Dingwall there was no sign of the cylinder cover. It was located long afterwards doing duty as a drinking dish for hens near Fodderty Junction.

In the autumn of 1917 the Allies had their backs to the wall. The threat of a German naval advance down the North Sea was imminent and to combat this menace it was decided to construct the Northern Barrage – a defence belt of mines extending across the North Sea. In the furtherance of this enterprise the Skye railway played a key role.

The base for the operation was at Dalmore, near Invergordon. In October 1917 a large distillery at that place was taken over by the Admiralty and converted into a mine assembly depot and store. At the same time the Admiralty took possession of all pier and transport facilities at Kyle of Lochalsh, which was to be the port of entry for the mines, and prepared the installations in readiness for the arrival of the United States naval personnel who were to conduct the operation. New sidings and loops were provided along the railway and the signalling was improved to give increased line capacity. Notice was given that civilian services on the line would be liable to severe restrictions and that only government freight would be accepted for transit through Kyle to the islands.

The first consignment of mines arrived from America in May 1918 and the traffic continued at roughly fortnightly intervals until November. On the arrival of a freighter three or four special trains were dispatched from Kyle for Dalmore daily for seven or eight days. Although the public timetables continued to advertise a full passenger service there were periods when there were paths for only one passenger train a day in each direction. The military trains were made up to a maximum of 11 wagons usually 12-ton coal wagons from a batch of 150 on loan from the South Eastern & Chatham

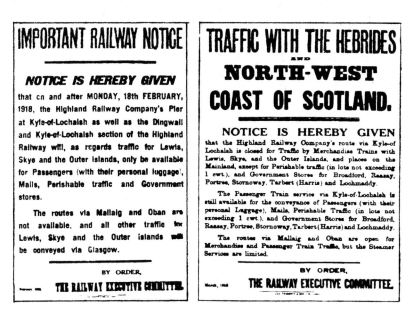

Traffic restrictions placed on the Skye line in World War I to allow transit of US mines for the Northern Barrage.

Railway. Four locomotives from the London & South Western Railway supplemented indigenous motive power.

During the operation 32,800 tons were carried along the Skye railway of which 24,000 tons went to Dalmore in about 400 special trains. As well as mine components the traffic included such diverse items as equipment for US hospitals in Britain, motor cars, hydraulic chairs for US army barbers' shops and cartons of chewing gum.

THE 1918 REPORT

In February 1918, with the outcome of World War I still in doubt, the Government appointed the Rural Transport (Scotland) Committee whose task it was to investigate ways of improving rural transport in the coming post war era. Special emphasis was given to providing railways in hitherto rail-less districts.

The Government was outstandingly frank in admitting that certain areas had been shamefully neglected in the past and the appointment of the committee was an act of penitence and atonement for the shortcomings of previous administrations. The proposed new railways 'will make good a defect in the whole system as it has been handed on to us by an earlier generation,' the committee observed. 'The railways have been recommended in some cases as making up a deficiency in the planning of previous generations which might have provided more districts with more railways as part of a general scheme for dealing with the whole country without a net addition to the total cost by providing lines of real utility.' The report went on to observe that it would not have been necessary to make apologies 'if the area of the north west Highlands had been allowed the opportunity of an orderly development which other hill districts in Europe such as Switzerland and other Alpine regions have enjoyed'. Nor was the social function of the railways overlooked. 'The inhabitants of these districts have a right to improved communications in the same way that they have a right to cheap postage'. The reporters saw little future in road transport:

The majority of the roads of the north of Scotland are unsuitable for heavy mechanically-propelled vehicles. The roadbed is weak and narrow and the drainage defective and under the destructive effect of heavy solid motor tyres is sooner or later worn into deep and dangerous ruts. The process is accelerated by the prevailing dampness of the climate which tends to keep the surface of the roads moist. To fit the roads for heavy traffic would probably entail an initial outlay of about £2000 per mile and the maintenance charges would always be heavy. The making of improved roads would cost nearly as much as the construction of a narrow gauge light railway.

The high cost of motor transport in the Highlands was spotlighted. The committee quoted an example of coal delivered at Lairg on the north line at 30s a ton and £5 being added for transporting it across country to Lochinver a distance of 48 miles. The reporters ruled out road transport as a means of transporting fish: 'Through the absence of rapid means of transit the greater part of the catch (in the Minches) has to be cured instead of being sent to the markets fresh. For the latter object to be realised railway termini north of Kyle are required.'

The omens had never been better for railway expansion in the north west. The old Skye line schemes were examined afresh. While the Achnasheen-Aultbea line was rejected as being too close to Kyle the Garve-Ullapool railway was acclaimed. Apart from the fact that this line would provide the shortest route from the fishing grounds to Inverness there was abundant water power around Ullapool which could be harnessed to support the new industrial development that the railway would bring to the area.

Skye was seen as a northern Anglesey with Dunvegan playing the role of Holyhead. Dunvegan in future would be the port for Stornoway and the outer island steamers. Passengers arriving by boat would join a train which would travel down through the island to a junction from which one branch would strike towards Kyleakin and a train ferry for Kyle of Lochalsh while another branch would proceed to Ardvasar and the ferry for Mallaig. Portree would be served by the railway and the Portree mailboat dispensed with, as would the internal bus service. 'The present motor buses from Portree to Uig and Dunvegan', said the report, 'are condemned for cutting up the roads, and for being uncomfortable in summer when they are crowded and in winter when all their passengers are exposed to all the blasts and all the rain.'

At the end of the war large quantities of military railway material, including 450 miles of unused narrow gauge track, became available for purchase. In February 1919 a deputation from the committee visited the main military railway workshops at Beaurainville in France and found a large force of German prisoners of war engaged in the repair of 500 engines of American, British and German origin, some 45 engines having already been completed and tested in steam. The deputation thought that a Baldwin 4–6–0 would handle 60 tons on the 1 in 50 gradients of the Garve-Ullapool line. Bearing in mind that freight would have to be trans-shipped from narrow to standard gauge at Garve the deputation inspected the operation of the trans-shipment point near Arras.

The committee set down its ideas on how the railways should be operated:

> The trains should be run at a low speed and in most cases the lines would be unfenced. The rolling stock should be adapted to passengers entering the carriages from the ends and at the level of the rails so that raised platforms would not be required. Fares would be collected en route thereby dispensing with booking clerks and booking offices. Instead of stations there would be halts or stopping places without buildings save where sheds were needed for the reception of goods waiting delivery or dispatch. It is recommended in all cases, with the exception of the proposed line to Lochinver, that these rural railways should be worked by one engine in steam thus avoiding the cost of signalling. A rural railway of this type would serve the needs of the district for purposes of development and its cost would be reduced to the minimum.

The matter was never put to the test. Not only did the war leave behind a flotsam of locomotives and railway materials but road vehicles by the thousand flooded the market. Men with new-found driving and mechanical skills bought surplus vehicles and set up in business as carriers serving local communities. The country bus came into its own. New road maintenance techniques made the lot of the road operator easier than ever it had been before. The established railway companies which in a different atmosphere might have sponsored the light railways were unsettled by the massive political changes – the grouping – looming ahead and were in no mood to embark on expensive adventures. Had they but known, the age of railway expansion was over. Very soon the railway would be on the defensive. The vision of Baldwins threading their way along 46 miles of magnificent narrow gauge railway in Skye or battling up to Braemore summit from the coast remained a dream, unfulfilled.

CHAPTER 8

LMS Days and After

The war left the Skye railway with a greater line capacity than it had enjoyed at any time in its history. The Highland purchased Loan loop from the Admiralty for £2000 and the naval sidings at Kyle for £650. Two Admiralty buildings at Kyle were acquired and converted into dwelling houses for the chief goods clerk and a craneman, and several wartime huts were put to use as offices and bothies. The timetables soon resumed a peacetime look. The winter timetable of 1922 offered three services each way on weekdays, the up trains leaving Kyle of Lochalsh at 7.0 am (goods), 11.0am (passenger) and 4.30pm (mixed), the down trains departing from Dingwall at 10.10am (mixed), 11.45am (passenger) and 3.45pm (mixed). That timetable was the last issued by the Highland Railway From 1 January 1923 control of the Skye railway passed from Inverness to London.

An indication of the attitude of the London Midland & Scottish Railway to its far-flung outpost in the Highlands was given when the ruling powers sent to the line an LNWR 2–4–0 to relieve a temporary engine shortage. That was turning the clock back with a vengeance! The engine lasted two days. The line remained a backwater well into LMS days. Apart from the fact that the engines and carriages slowly shed their Highland green for LMS maroon the railway changed very little. One wonders what the LMS hierarchy must have thought when they learned that the residents in their hotel at Kyle of Lochalsh still went to bed carrying candles. In September 1931 the Controller of Hotels found that 'the lighting of the Station Hotel at Kyle of Lochalsh by lamps and candles is adversely commented

140

on by the guests'. He recommended the purchase of a second-hand generator. The equipment was duly installed but it did not function during the night because it generated noise as well as electricity. The Post Office and the National Bank of Scotland took current from the installation, the hotel thus functioning as a power station on the side.

Shunting at Kyle pier was contracted to Wordie & Co of Glasgow the well-known railway carriers and was accomplished by horse power. A report on an accident involving Andrew Stewart, whose official designation was 'shunting horseman' throws light on shunting procedure.

On the west pier there were two lines. The 'main' line ended in a short dock with accommodation for two wagons. At a point just short of the dock a second line diverged, the junction being controlled by a pair of hand points. On the day of the accident Stewart was placing wagons in position convenient for the transfer of freight to the steamers. The dock already contained its limit of two wagons. When Stewart approached the points leading a third wagon it was his intention to place it on the seaward track. But by some mischance the points had not been reset and he found himself with his horse trapped in the rapidly diminishing space between the moving wagons and the stationary wagons in the dock. Stewart quickly unhitched his horse and pushed it clear and in so doing left himself with insufficient time to escape. He was crushed between the buffers and killed instantly.

A lady who had the misfortune to be standing almost at the point of impact gave a graphic account of the occurrence at the subsequent fatal accident inquiry:

> I saw a man shunting wagons. He was working with a horse and I saw him from where I stood close to the railway turning table. He was leading a horse pulling a wagon along the line. There was a stationary wagon at the end of the line. Some little distance before he came to the stationary wagon he put the horse clear of the rails, but before he got clear of the rails himself the wagon which the horse had been pulling ran into the stationary wagon and Stewart was crushed between the buffers.

Some indication of the speed at which the shunting operation was conducted is shown by the fact that the wagon rebounded

12ft after the impact. The stationmaster, asked if he considered the procedure dangerous replied that it had been in operation for many years without mishap. Stewart, although not a railway employee, had been entirely responsible for working the points. The jury returned a verdict of accidental death concluding that the victim had failed to set the points correctly.

Another accident which occurred at Garve on 23 December 1926 sheds more light on an aspect of train working on the Skye line. The train involved was the afternoon mixed from Dingwall to Kyle, the misdeeds of which have already been chronicled in earlier pages. The rails were sheathed in frost and when the train left Garve the right hand sander on the engine was out of action. Almost at once the left hand sander failed and the engine lost its feet, slipping badly on the rising gradient. The driver sent his fireman forward to clear the left hand sander, and while he was fumbling in the darkness with the sander pipe the engine moved forward and a wheel severed two of his fingers. The train set back to Garve and when another fireman had been obtained the train resumed its journey this time with both sanders working. But such were the conditions that the engine could not get a bite on the rail and the train returned to Garve again to reduce the load. The inspecting officer in his report commented: 'Engines working on the heavy gradients of the Dingwall-Kyle of Lochalsh line are supplied with sand which is so fine that it cakes readily on coming into contact with moisture at the bottom of the sand pipes, the result being that the pipes are frequently choked so that the men try to clear them while the engines are in motion. Moreover, this fine sand is not sufficiently effective as a preventative of slipping. The provision of sand that is coarser, containing more grit, is recommended.'

Raven Rock, which had added to locomotive coal consumption relentlessly over the years was not an unmitigated liability. The formation contained rock which, suitably processed made excellent road building material. Spurred by the road improvement boom which followed the war the Mid Ross District Committee decided to open a quarry at Raven's Rock. Since there was no road access to the site the local authority sought a rail connection to the proposed quarry which the Highland agreed to provide in May 1922. The scheme was re-authorised by the LMS a year later. The easiest approach to the quarry site would have been from the east but once again the whim of a landowner shaped the pattern of events. To preserve his estate from the sight and sound of quarrying he decreed that access must be from the west side of the Rock. This meant that the stone had to be worked against the grain which made it difficult for the quarrymen to maintain a vertical face. An experienced quarryman was brought in from Aberdeen to take charge of the workings.

A siding controlled by a ground frame at the west end of Raven Rock cutting gave access to the quarry. The points faced west and empty wagons were propelled into the sidings. The ground frame was operated by an Annett's key which the driver obtained from the stationmaster at Achterneed. Five sidings, two of which passed under the crushers, opened out from the main siding on the quarry floor, these being under the control of the quarry foreman and operated by the same Annett's key provided for Raven Rock ground frame. Catch points at the quarry gates protected the main line.

In its peak years the quarry employed a quarrymaster and 20 men, and produced 120 tons of processed stone a day. Normally a train of 10 loaded wagons was dispatched daily at a time decided by the Achterneed stationmaster. On occasions the load was stepped up to 12 vehicles, and in the late LMS period it became 16. The wagons were taken to Dingwall to be marshalled for destinations mainly in the Highlands.

Access to the quarry for workers was by a cycle track situated on the south side of the line between Achterneed and Raven Rock. The uphill journey was hard going and the men were in the habit of stealing rides on freight trains until a fatal accident put an end to the practice. By all accounts the homeward journey from work was an exhilarating affair. The cyclists whizzed down the 1 in 50 vying with each other to break records and sometimes their speed bettered that of the trains. The best time is said to have been six minutes for the five mile course.

Apart from its main function the Raven Rock Annett's key

served as a token for engines banking trains up to the summit, a duty usually performed by the Dingwall pilot. The procedure was for the pilot to be coupled on to the rear of the train at Dingwall with a stop at Achterneed to uncouple. The engine subsequently dropped off at Raven Rock and returned light to Dingwall. The quarry ceased to be worked after June 1939, but the sidings were not removed until 1952. The Annett's key continued in use for the banking engines until Achterneed signal box was closed in 1966.

It was not until after the first world war that Kyle of Lochalsh had a local council. The first council chamber was the station waiting room and railwaymen were among the first legislators. They tell the story of the station foreman who proposed that Kyle should have a district nurse and proceeded to marry the good lady when she arrived. Kyle prospered in the inter-war years. The village became the commercial and social centre for a wide area. An oil depot was established from which fuel for heating, lighting and propulsion was distributed to the islands. Many of the old black houses – windowless cottages with thick stone walls – shed their thatch for corrugated iron, but the womenfolk still came to Kyle as they had done in the first days of the railway to barter their produce at the local stores. A traveller thus described the arrival of the morning train at Kyle in 1924:

> Out flocked the women from Duirinish, Plockton and Strome carrying baskets of butter, eggs and some homespun. These they traded at the Pioneer Store in return for provisions and one returning passenger had a half bag of meal on her broad shoulders.

In August 1929 the LMS decided, not without trepidation, to run the first ever Sunday excursion train from Inverness to Kyle. There were ominous rumblings in the district and the company expected trouble, for the spirit that had inspired the Battle of Strome Pier was by no means dead. What happened was told in a letter to a friend by the motive power inspector who accompanied the train:

> We had a very good train – 285 passengers. I could fine have stayed at home as I have plenty of running about during the week, but the Wee Frees were vowing vengeance on us if we dared to come to Kyle on a

Sunday so I did not want to let them think that I was afraid to come. However, everything was very quiet when we arrived. No one took any notice and we had a splendid day.

The passengers that day had hoped to set foot in Skye but the ferryman refused to carry them. Two years later a railway employee collapsed and died shortly after the departure of an excursion train from Kyle. The incident was blamed on the Sunday train and on the matter being raised in Parliament the LMS was advised to use discretion in selecting destinations for its Sunday trains in future.

Very successful through excursions were instituted between Elgin, Forres, Nairn and Inverness to Kyle but they were run on week-days only. Between 18 April and 15 September the LMS ran 39 half-day excursions in the Highland area of which six had Kyle of Lochalsh as their destination. In 1933 out of a total of 48 excursions nine went to Kyle while in 1934 15 of the 59 excursions were advertised for Kyle. The list of excursions was made up in February of each year, the official responsible having to consult the tide tables as well as his working timetable. Trains arriving at Kyle near low water were marked on the list and the advertising department was cautioned not to mention the opportunity for the passengers to visit Skye on such occasions.

Timetables remained little altered during the LMS period, but loads increased as more powerful engines appeared on the line. According to an LMS route availability book dated 1945 the only ex-Highland engine barred from the Skye railway was the Class 3F 0–6–0. When the Cumming Clan Goods 4–6–0s were sent to the line the turntable at Kyle had to be lengthened to take them, a process which involved the excavation of more rock from the perimeter of the turntable pit. The Highland engines were followed by the LMS Class 5 4–6–0s, the finest machine the Skye line men had ever handled. During part of the LMS period some colour was brought to operations by the naming of the two main boat trains *The Hebridean* and *The Hebrides*.

Strathpeffer never regained its pre-war glory. By 1929 the company that ran the Spa was £3000 in debt and patronage was

L M S
LONDON MIDLAND AND SCOTTISH RAILWAY

Glasgow Weekly Herald

DAY EXCURSION

OVER THE SEA TO SKYE

On Tuesday night, 19th July, 1932

Outward Journey.		Tuesday night.		Return Journey.		Wed's'day night.	
		p.m.				p.m.	
Glasgow (Buchanan Street)	leave	11 50	Portree (Steamer)	leave		8	15
		Wed's'day	Broadford (Steamer)	,,		9	25
		morning.	Kyle of Lochalsh (Steamer)	arrive		10	0
Stirling	leave	12 35a	,, ,,	leave		10	30
Perth	,,	1 30	Plockton	,,		10	42
Forres	,,	5 0	Strome Ferry	,,		10	54
Nairn	,,	5 25	Strathcarron	,,		11	12
Inverness	arrive	5 45	Achnasheen	,,		11	50
,,	leave	6 5				Thursday	
Dingwall	,,	6 40				morning.	
Garve	,,	7 20	Garve	,,		12	28a
Achnasheen	,,	7 50	Dingwall	,,		12	51
Strathcarron	,,	8 25	Inverness	arrive		1	35
Strome Ferry	,,	8 45	,,	leave		1	45
Plockton	,,	8 55	Nairn	,,		2	8
Kyle of Lochalsh	arrive	9 7	Forres	,,		2	26
,, ,, (Steamer)	leave	9 35	Perth	arrive		6	12
Broadford (Steamer)	arrive	10 25	Stirling	,,		7	15
Portree (Steamer)	,,	11 30	Glasgow (Buchanan Street)	,,		8	5

RETURN FARE   22/-   GLASGOW TO SKYE

The First Day Excursion Glasgow to Skye

PLEASE RETAIN THIS PROGRAMME FOR REFERENCE   [SEE OVER

The First Day Excursion Glasgow to Skye. The special train conveyed a dining car and sleeping cars Glasgow to Kyle of Lochalsh. Sleeping berths cost 6s each way and full breakfasts and hot suppers were served at 2s 6d each. On arrival at Portree the excursionists had the choice of a cruise by launch or a circular tour of the island by coach. The complete tour, including all fares, sleeping berths and four meals cost £3 2s 6d.

dwindling. The proprietors urged the LMS to purchase and operate the Spa, the argument being that a refurbished Spa would bring extra traffic to the railway. The LMS had no illusions on the subject. It was appreciated in the boardroom that most visitors to the Spa now came by road, a fact which did not unduly perturb the company since it had been prudent enough under its policy of 'Withdrawal of Passenger Train Services and Relinquishment of Passengers to Associated Omnibus Companies' to acquire shares to the value of £14,000 in the Inverness & District Motor Car Company. What the LMS was losing on the roundabouts it was gaining on the swings. Nevertheless the LMS was aware that many of the patrons of its own hotel in Strathpeffer were attracted to the resort by the Spa and it was to save the hotel rather than the railway that the LMS entered into negotiations with the Spa proprietors. Company engineers inspected the equipment and samples of the water were sent to Derby for analysis. The water was pronounced to be good but the equipment was found to be much more decrepit than expected. The LMS abandoned all thoughts of acquiring the Spa. Henceforward the company concentrated on promoting their Lochalsh Hotel. In 1938 it earned £8873 compared with £8417 earned by the much larger Highland Hotel at Strathpeffer.

In September 1939 the Skye railway once more found itself placed on a war footing and for the next six years the scenes of 1914–18 were re-enacted. The threat to southern ports by enemy bombers resulted in naval activity being concentrated in the relatively safe waters of the west coast lochs and inlets, and the railway became more vital to the nation than it had been even in World War 1. Once again loops were put in, engines borrowed and long, heavily-loaded trains, mostly naval, became the order of the day between Dingwall and Kyle.

One afternoon in November 1940 the 11.45am from Inverness to Kyle was held at Strome Ferry for no immediately apparent reason. It stayed there for nearly four hours during which a drama was being fought out at the terminus. Had things gone the wrong way there might have been no Kyle of Lochalsh by nightfall.

On that day, as on most days, the sidings and pier at Kyle were stacked with explosives. On the east pier were at least 20 wagons of mines, and elsewhere in the immediate area were 30 vans loaded with depth charges, detonators and other implements of war waiting to be loaded into vessels. Moored to a buoy ½ mile off the pier the minelayer *Port Napier* with 500 mines already aboard was taking oil from a tanker before sailing on a mission.

Shortly after noon the *Port Napier* was seen to be burning. If she blew up and the explosion detonated all the explosives in the vicinity, the effect, in the mountain-girt strait, hardly bore thinking about. The village was evacuated. The mail boats and naval vessels tied up at the piers scattered. Naval personnel and LMS staff began to clear the pier of potentially dangerous traffic. It was no easy task. Some of the wagons had already been positioned alongside vessels and they had to be hand-shunted across turnplates and through points. Eventually all were drawn into the deep railway cutting beyond the station.

During the afternoon there was an explosion aboard the burning ship but the mines did not go up. They burned and threw off clouds of acrid smoke which rose high above the tops of the Skye hills. At length the vessel sank leaving a patch of burning oil on the water. The danger to Kyle was over.

With the end of the war traffic reverted to normal. Nationalisation in 1948 brought little outward sign of change. In time a redundant observation car from the Southern Region Waterloo-Ilfracombe *Devon Belle* Pullman train was brought north in an attempt to stimulate the tourist traffic. The summer through traffic to the islands flourished. A dining car was attached to the morning down train and at Achnasheen transferred to the up train. It was not uncommon to see two double-headed boat trains and a double-headed freight, all the engines being Class 5s, within station limits. Strathpeffer was closed to passengers on 2 March 1946. The branch continued to be used mainly for coal traffic until 26 March 1951 when it was closed completely. On 1 May 1954 Lochluichart station was closed along with two miles of track in the immediate vicinity. The Conon Valley hydro electric project called for the raising of

the RAIL road to the isles ...

between INVERNESS and KYLE of LOCHALSH

See the Mountains and Glens in the armchair comfort of the

BUFFET OBSERVATION CAR

OBSERVATION CAR SERVICES

Inverness to Kyle of Lochalsh
3rd May until 2nd October

Inverness	leave	10 40
Kyle of Lochalsh	arrive	13 40

Kyle of Lochalsh to Inverness
3rd May to 2nd October

Kyle of Lochalsh	leave	17 30
Inverness	arrive	20 30

Daily (except Sundays) 3rd May to 2nd October, 1965

This luxury car, with large windows and comfortable seats, is attached to the rear of the trains shown above.

Accommodation can be reserved in advance at Inverness Station for the journey to Kyle of Lochalsh and at Kyle of Lochalsh Station for the journey to Inverness.

SUPPLEMENTARY CHARGE FOR THE SINGLE JOURNEY IN EITHER DIRECTION

5/-

Light refreshments can be obtained in the Observation Car.

British Railways handbill advertising the former Devon Belle observation car run on the Kyle of Lochalsh line in the 1960s. One of the two observation cars of this type survive in Britain on the privately-run Dart Valley Railway in Devon, giving passengers views of the glorious scenery bordering the River Dart.

149

Loch Luichart by 25ft and that involved the flooding of the railway and the station. The stationmaster's house and
surfacemen's cottages, still paraffin-lit and as primitive as on
the day when they were grudgingly built by the Dingwall &
Skye, disappeared under the water. The new station and formation were brought into use on 3 May 1954. Part of the old
formation is visible at the western end of the deviation. In
winter there was little difference between the pattern of 1955
and that of 1875. William Whitelaw once told the Highland
shareholders that their railway would be a highly profitable
concern if it were kept open for the four summer months and
closed completely during the remaining eight months of the
year. His remark applied in great measure to the Skye railway
through four changes of ownership.

THE KYLEAKIN FERRY

The Highland Railway placed great importance on the development of the ferry link between Kyle of Lochalsh and Kyleakin. On 4 May 1897 the general manager stated that he was
negotiating with David MacBrayne for the provision of a
steamboat on the crossing, and on 1 October 1897, a month
before the opening of the Kyle extension, the engineer reported,
'The steam ferry can be opened to public traffic on the same day
as the line to Kyle'. The poster advertising the opening of the
line promised that a steam ferry would connect the mainland
with Skye. But when the first passengers stepped out of the
train at Kyle all they found on the ferry crossing was a gabbart –
a small rowing boat. Many years were to pass before a more
substantial craft was provided. The Kyle-Portree steamer provided the main link with Skye.

    Although it was not realised at the time, the coming of the
motor car held promise for the future of the ferry. But motor
cars were primitive and few, the roads were bad and a journey
to the west coast more a penance than a pleasure. From
Strathcarron the road to the west followed the north shore of
Loch Carron as far as Strome Inn. There the traveller had to
find Murdo Macleod the tenant of the inn who as part of his

tenancy was obliged to ferry travellers across Loch Carron to
Strome Ferry. From there the route to Kyle was over the hills to
Glenelg and through Balmacara. The crossing of the strait was
an adventure in itself and beyond Kyleakin unspeakable roads
led into the interior of the island.

In November 1910 the gabbart was declared unsafe, and
John Macdonald, boatbuilder of Oban, was commissioned to
build a new boat at a cost of only £8 5s. This unpretentious
vessel carried passengers, sheep, the occasional cow and very
rarely a motor car. There seemed to be two ways of dealing with
cars; either the vehicle was loaded on to the boat with substantial parts overhanging the water, or it was placed on a barge
and towed across. In either event the passage was hazardous, a
fact acknowledged by the Highland Railway which insured
every vehicle making the crossing. The policy, with Car & General, was good for 50 crossings with one car at a time. The ferryman was obliged to keep a record and inform the manager
when 40 cars had crossed so that the policy could be renewed. It
was all very primitive, yet here was the genesis of an idea that in
time was to revolutionise inter-island transport.

It was not until 1918 that a motor boat was placed on the service. It was a Kelvin 13/15hp launch built by the Bergius
Launch Company of Glasgow at a cost of £459 0s 10d. It could
carry 12 passengers, as well as sheep, goods and one car. In an
average year the ferry catered for 600 passengers and 40 cars. In
1917, when traffic had been below average, 24 cars, 2000 sheep
and 50 head of cattle were carried. Fares varied from 2d for a
sheep and 6d for a passenger to £1 for a car. In 1921 a second
although smaller motor boat was obtained and in the following
year a rowing boat costing £19 was added to the fleet. Alexander Newlands, the Highland Railway engineer, was responsible for the hulls of the vessels, but the ferry operations were
the responsibility of local contractors who also had to pay for
crews and engine maintenance. The contractors paid an
annual rental to the railway company for the ferry rights and
retained the receipts. In December 1922, at the end of the Highland Railway era, there were four crossings daily; additional
crossings could be arranged on payment of a special fee.

In 1927 the Chief Marine Superintendent of the LMS on a visit to Kyle expressed dismay at the primitive methods used to run the ferry. He insisted that the towing of a gabbart loaded with a car, and sometimes freight and livestock, was unacceptable and he recommended that a self-propelled boat be obtained from Webster & Bickerton of Goole. The new boat was fitted with a 30hp engine.

In October 1934 John Clark, who had been the ferry lessee for many years, intimated that he did not wish to continue. The ferry rights were leased to the David MacBrayne Trust for an annual rental of £150 and one third of the receipts. That was an astute move on the part of the railway company. The LMS had a half share in MacBraynes so that not only did it collect the rental and one third of the receipts but also half of the remaining two-thirds. The first year of the MacBrayne operation – 1935 – was rewarding for all concerned. The receipts for the year were £5462 of which £3470 was clear profit.

As the popularity and profitability of the ferry increased steps were taken to improve facilities. The efficiency of the operation was diminished because the ferry slipways were unusable at low tide and long delays were endemic. In 1935 negotiations were begun with the local authorities with a view to having the slipways extended. The Kyle of Lochalsh slipway was owned by Ross & Cromarty County Council and the slipway at Kyleakin by Inverness County Council and great difficulty was experienced in finding a scheme which suited both parties. It was not until the second world war had begun that work on the slipways was completed. Meanwhile a new boat capable of taking two cars at a time had been obtained. The LMS attracted extra traffic to the ferry by carrying motor cars and their passengers from Strathcarron to Kyle by train, thereby cutting out the daunting road journey. During the second world war, when the Kyle-Portree mailboat service was cancelled, the ferry became the principal means of communication between the mainland and Skye. In 1942 when a new boat was called for in a hurry the engines were completed in 10 weeks, and the hull was available two weeks later. With the steady increase in road traffic over the years each new generation of ferry boat became larger and more efficient. The modern roll-on roll-off ferries now convey 350,000 cars a year

THREAT OF CLOSURE

The Skye railway must have looked a tempting morsel to Dr Beeching when he pored over his maps planning the decimation of the British railway system. Here was a line straggling over $63\frac{1}{2}$ of the most barren miles in the kingdom. If ever a railway was ripe for the pruning knife it was the Skye railway.

But the Skye line escaped the Beeching dismemberment. It was seen as an expensive but necessary line of communication with the island communities. Nevertheless, by 1970, far-reaching changes planned for communications in the area threatened the obliteration of the railway. A new road designed to bypass Strome Ferry and give easier road access to Kyle of Lochalsh was being built parallel to the railway, along the shore of Loch Carron between Strathcarron and Strome. Official policy envisaged the upgrading of the Garve-Ullapool road and the emergence of Ullapool as the mainland port for Stornoway. A large passenger and vehicle ferry was under construction and when ready would provide a twice daily shuttle between Ullapool and Stornoway, express buses providing the link to Inverness. Further it was expected that the Portree mail boat would be withdrawn and the traffic it handled would be handed over to road traffic with a high proportion of the vehicles crossing by the Kyleakin ferry and continuing their journey on the new or improved mainland roads.

There was an ominous moment in November 1969 when blasting operations for the new road near Attadale precipitated a rockfall which completely blocked the railway. Four years earlier a rockfall had resulted in the premature closure of the eastern half of the Callander & Oban Railway. Passengers for Kyle of Lochalsh from Inverness were taken by bus via Loch Ness, Glen Moriston and Glen Shiel. It was not until 13 March 1970 that the line between Strathcarron and Strome Ferry was re-opened and through services between Inverness and Kyle partly restored. The 10.30am from Inverness and the 11.08am and 5.30pm services from Kyle were resumed, but the 4.55am boat connection to Kyle continued to be worked by bus via Loch Ness. The 5.40pm terminated at Achnasheen, passengers for Achnashellach and Strathcarron being taken forward by local bus. The period of enforced road transport was watched with interest by those people who regarded the railway as their lifeline. They were not displeased to note that the replacement buses not only took longer on the journey but were less reliable than the trains.

Attadale proved as difficult an obstacle to the road engineers as it had been to Murdoch Paterson a century earlier. The solution was a concrete avalanche shelter which covered both road and railway at the point most threatened. Steel-meshed netting stretched over the cliff faces east and west of the shelter tamed the tumbling rocks.

Even after trains were restored the grim situation was that the Skye railway seemed about to lose the prime reason for its existence. It came as no surprise when in December 1971 the Secretary of State for Scotland consented to the closure of the line, albeit with a stay of execution until 31 December 1973. In 1972 the line cost £318,000 to run and earned £51,000, leaving a deficit of £267,000. Its best friends had to concede that, deprived of the boat traffic, it would be providing a very expensive service for a very few people. Nevertheless, the Skye line had friends and was to make many more in the months immediately ahead.

Between 1950 and 1972 just under 4000 miles of Scotland's 7391 miles of railway had been closed – about half the national network. There had been protests and plans for preservation in plenty but only one threatened line – the East Kilbride branch – had won a reprieve. With the Skye line matters were different. The threat to the railway took place at a time of resurgent Scottish nationalism and the destruction of the railway was seen as a national affront. The public at large, local authorities, Members of Parliament and bodies like the Highlands & Islands Development Board and the Scottish Association for Public Transport rallied to its support. People who could not have pointed out the line on a map joined the campaign. The railway even had a following south of the Border.

The people who had most to lose fought hardest. A storekeeper in Kyle refused to accept delivery of goods that arrived by road, pointing out to the consignors that it was cheaper to route their traffic by rail. One protest meeting at Kyle was opened by the minister praying: 'Lord protect us from the machinations of those who would take away our railway'. Local people tended to talk of *our* railway not *the* railway.

The Skye line basked in publicity on a scale it had never known in its lifetime. People came from far and near to see the railway for themselves. They came in hundreds at a time by ordinary train and chartered train. On 13 June 1970 the Great North of Scotland Railway Association ran a special train from Aberdeen to Kyle of Lochalsh with 360 passengers. Interest in the line was such that the trip had to be repeated. In the following year the Association ran three trips from Aberdeen to Kyle, all fully booked. The idea was catching. In 1972 the *Evening Express* of Aberdeen ran four trips to Kyle the profits going to various charities. Among other local organisations which took to the iron road to the isles were the Liberal Party, Stoneywood Works, the National Association of Local Government Officers, the RAF Association and the Heart and Lung Foundation.

Meanwhile special trains were arriving at Kyle from more distant centres. British Rail, following the lead of the enthusiasts, put on day trips from Edinburgh, while the Scottish Railway Preservation Society organised tours from Glasgow, Larbert, Stirling and Perth. It was a novelty for Lowlanders to be able to go to Kyle and back in a day with the prospect of putting a foot briefly on Skye. The distance from Glasgow to Kyle and back is 528 miles and the SRPS trains normally consisted of 11 coaches with all seats taken and a hundred or so passengers left behind. On 18 September 1971 the *Hebridean Express* organised by the Wirral Railway Circle ran to Kyle all the way from Crewe. The *Hebridean Express* returned again twice in 1973. On the occasion of the April 1973 visit the Wirral Railway Circle also sent *The Jacobite* to Mallaig, and the passengers changed trains by the Kyle-Mallaig steamer. For that excursion, with Crewe again the starting point, 17 diesel locomotives, 2 restaurant cars, 8 sleeping cars and 22 other carriages were employed and 800 people passed through Kyle.

All that feverish activity took place against a background of apprehension. The Government gave no indication that the line would be retained after the expiry of the two years of grace. By mid-summer of 1973 the SRPS was advertising a valedictory tour of the line to take place from Glasgow on the last Saturday of December.

A PRAYER ANSWERED

At this point a new factor appeared – oil-related industry. A plan had been put forward for the establishment of an oil rig platform site at Drumbuie near Kyle. With a major industry in the area the future of the railway would be secure, but at dire cost to the environment. The local people fought as vehemently to keep the oilmen out as they fought to keep the railway in. *The Scotsman* had this to say of the situation:

> Oil is an uncertain ally for the Kyle campaigners. The project for building oil platforms near Kyle has run into heavy opposition. It may or may not earn the Secretary of State's approval, but even if it does not a harbour and railhead at Kyle should be worth keeping, to serve developments elsewhere on the west coast. But the case for the Kyle line should not be founded mainly on oil. It passes through splendid scenery; passenger traffic has been increasing in the past two years and should be capable of further expansion, especially if public interest is stimulated by attractions like steam locomotive excursions. With imagination the Kyle line could be given a magnetic appeal. If oil has persuaded the authorities to re-assess the future of the line its other uses and potentialities should reinforce the case for prolonging its life indefinitely.

The Ullapool-Stornoway steamer service began on 26 March 1973 when the Skye railway lost a steamer connection it had maintained for 103 years. Usually one bus was sufficient to cope with passengers travelling from Inverness to Ullapool for the boat and passenger traffic on the Kyle line was little affected. But the lorries rumbling along the Ullapool road bound for the twice daily ferries made heavy inroads on Kyle line freight.

During the summer of 1973 no one in Inverness could have remained unaware of the existence of the line. A banner hung across the station frontage invited populace and visitors to 'Explore Your Scenic Line'. Attractive, well-designed pamphlets were distributed. The Skye railway was given a stag's head logo which appeared on literature and posters. The logo also appeared on an attractive and inexpensive Skye line tie introduced by BR and sold with the tickets at the booking office. A splendid film of the line was produced and shown to MPs and peers at Westminster before being released for public exhibition.

Between Easter and the end of September 1973 Ross and Cromarty County Council conducted its own survey to establish how many people travelled on the line, who they were, and why they were in the trains. In July and August the trains carried an average of 200 passengers, but the number fell to 100 and less during the spring and autumn months. Tourists formed the overwhelming bulk of the traffic. Residents in the vicinity of the stations and people in the hamlets connected to the railway by buses and motor launches used the trains sparingly; residents of Skye hardly at all. The line had ceased to perform the function for which it had been built – to provide an easy route for Skyemen travelling to Inverness and the South. Nevertheless, the report made it abundantly clear that without the railway the district's only industry – tourism – would die.

The summer and autumn of 1973 passed, and winter began without a decision having been announced on the future of the railway. Then on 2 November Mr William Hamilton, Member of Parliament for West Fife initiated a debate on the future of Scottish railways. Referring to Mr Keith Speed, Under Secretary of State for the Environment, Mr Hamilton observed:

If the Hon Gentleman can make some statement on the Kyle of Lochalsh line which is under threat of closure by the end of this year, I hope he will give that favourable consideration. It would be a tragedy if that line were to be slaughtered. It has great tourist potential and with some financial help from the oil companies as suggested to me by the Labour candidate for Ross & Cromarty, it could be saved.

Mr Speed's reply held momentous news for the Highlands:

> The Hon Gentleman has asked me about the Inverness-Kyle of Lochalsh line and made some interesting comments about it. After full consultation with the Secretary of State for Scotland, consent for closure was given in December 1971 on condition that the service should not be withdrawn until the beginning of 1974, and then only after specific replacement bus services had been provided.
>
> There has been considerable development in the concrete oil platform industry and in oil exploration off the coast of Britain since that decision was taken. We considered carefully whether recent developments could justify the retention of the passenger service. We had particularly in mind the possibility that the line could be used to transport heavy freight if there were to be major oil developments on the west coast.
>
> My Hon Friend, the Member for Ross & Cromarty who is a Whip and silent in this Chamber, has not been silent outside. He has been conducting an energetic and forceful campaign, and I have seen him about the matter on a number of occasions. He has been putting consistently the point of view that it would be folly for the line to be closed at this stage.
>
> I am pleased to tell the Hon Gentleman that my Right Hon Friend the Minister for Transport Industries recently concluded that it would not be right to implement closure on 1 January 1974 even if arrangements for the replacement buses could have been made in time. He will instead be considering the line's future when we have a clearer view about future requirements for freight traffic. As he recently informed my Hon Friend the Member for Ross & Cromarty, the line will be kept open throughout 1974 so as to give ample time for a sound decision to be made in the light of the further assessment which he will be making. I hope that this will be welcomed in the area. We shall be further considering the matter with the Scottish Office and the Department of Trade & Industry.

A reprieve for a year! There was nothing about the railway during that year to indicate that the end might be nigh. Passengers came in ever-increasing numbers. There was a spirit of optimism abroad. But in the end it was oil that saved the line. Permission was given for the construction of a concrete platform site at Loch Kishorn near the mouth of Loch Carron on its north side. The line clearly would be an important feeder. The threat that hung over the railway for so long was removed unconditionally. The *Courier and Advertiser* of Dundee spoke for every friend of the line:

> The Kyle rail line has escaped the axe. The Government have recognised the good sense of retaining a line that is an essential communication line in the Highlands. But their conversion from the old Beeching philosophy might have been too late if it hadn't been for the tenacity of local people and others who fought hard to keep the line. If people are determined enough they can make an impression on the Mandarins of Whitehall.

Kyle of Lochalsh. 37261 hauls the empty stock out of Kyle station 19 July 1985. Note the ex-engineers' saloon used as the observation saloon on a summer round trip from Inverness in the background. *W. A. Sharman*

Above: 37025 at platform 5 at Inverness with the 1755 for Kyle of Lochalsh on 28 June 1985. Note the station groundframe between the curving south and north platforms.

Below: 37114 arrives on 10 August 1985 with the 0710 ex-Kyle past one of the signal gantries now replaced by colour-light signalling. *Both W. A. Sharman*

Above: The traditional Kyle of Lochalsh shot showing 37414 with the regular 1645 departure and Sprinter 150205 on a special from Dundee on 30 April 1988.
Below: The same Sprinter representing the new, low-cost, order on the line *Both Alan Mitchell*

Hope forlorn. As explained in the new chapter 9, the oil-rig building yard at Strome Ferry did not after all provide the sustained freight traffic that John Thomas hoped would be the saviour of the line. The empty sidings and closed yard are seen as in April 1988. *Alan Mitchell*

Postscript

When the late John Thomas updated this book to 1975, he quite rightly attached great importance to the potential rail freight traffic arising from the establishment in that year of a concrete oil platform construction yard on a deep water site at Loch Kishorn. The prospect of large flows of steel, cement and fly ash (the last from Longannet Power Station) to be used at the yard, moving over the line as far as Strome Ferry where sidings were laid, seemed to be the saviour of the line for the foreseeable future. Coupled with the strongly expressed public feeling and political representation vividly portrayed by John Thomas in the previous chapter, this large-scale freight traffic set the seal on the campaign against closure, and caused a collective sigh of relief among residents and supporters.

The crucial point about the freight traffic was a condition attached to the granting of planning permission for the yard. This stipulated that it must be treated as an 'island site', with construction materials being brought in by sea. This meant that rail could compete more effectively with road, since both would involve transhipment to barges at some point, and the major advantage of site-to-site haulage often held by road transport would disappear.

Everything looked set for a resurgence of traffic to the Skye line and for a time in the mid and late 1970s freight passed through the sidings at Strome Ferry, being transhipped to barges for the trip across Lochs Carron and Kishorn to the construction yard. Then another twist in the line's history occurred: by the end of 1982 this traffic had ceased and the sidings had been disconnected from the running line. There was no longer a demand for concrete platforms and Highland Regional Council agreed to relax the 'island site' condition, the construction yard receiving most of its remaining materials by road. This blow has since been softened in retrospect, for the yard itself closed in 1986 due to a lack of orders, reflecting the uncertainty of the oil industry in the face of declining oil prices. An intriguing possibility of reopening arose in late 1987, when companies seeking contracts to build structures for the Channel Tunnel expressed interest in the Kishorn Yard, but this is now unlikely to lead to a return of freight traffic to Strome Ferry.

Despite these blows, the line survives and in some ways flourishes. Its future in the last years of the 20th century is perhaps as secure as it was at any time since the 1950s, despite the decline and virtual disappearance of freight traffic. The situation of the line for the foreseeable future involves three strands: the political context; a growth in passenger traffic, particularly tourism; and a reduction in operating costs.

The political context has its roots in the dismay that a line closure proposal would cause in Scotland generally and in the Highlands in particular. This has been the case since the 1950s, but the potential outcry could now be all the greater due to an increased public interest in what might be termed scenic rail travel and the wellbeing of remote areas. This is part of a broader awareness of the importance of our heritage and environment, and would ensure indignation beyond the Scottish border if any of the Highland railways were seriously threatened. Nevertheless, a determined government, or Railways Board, might make the attempt. However, the political stance of Scotland's voters would weigh against such a move, and most observers agree that for the present at least the political climate does not look like leading to serious closure proposals, notwithstanding severe financial pressure on ScotRail. There is, of course, always the possibility that this analysis is wrong, and one or more Highland lines could face a closure threat, probably with the intended mitigation of a 'bus replacement service'. In that event, it is to be hoped that the views on opposition, expressed above, would be vindicated.

Fortunately, more tangible trends can also be identified to support a moderately optimistic view of the line's future. These trends can be traced back to the summer season of 1983, when Sunday excursion trains were run between Inverness and Kyle. They were criticised by the Lord's Day Observance Society, and the Area Manager received some letters of personal damnation from clergymen, but the trains were an instant success.

Then, on 7 September 1983, the Inverness Area Business Group was formed with the aim of involving the railway's functional managers – Mechanical, Signalling and Civil Engineering, Operations, Train Crew and Personnel – in running the business at Area level. The main tasks of the Group were to obtain maximum revenue at minimum cost, and to provide the most attractive service possible to customers. The latter aim was reflected in the setting up of a 'Customer Care Panel'. As part of the effort to expand the passenger business, several attractively priced packages have been offered, including half day excursions from Inverness to Kyle, 'Rail and Sail' trips in conjunction with Caledonian MacBrayne, rail and bus trips in conjunction with Clan Coaches and, of course, the 'Grand Circular Tour' from Inverness to Fort William via Skye by rail and sea, returning to Inverness by bus.

The success of the Inverness Area Business Group has been seen in increased passenger numbers and revenue on the line, and is also visible in the Green and Cream (old Highland Railway) station repainting of 1984, together with new electric platform lighting and station re-signing. In 1986 the Provincial Sector of BR took over the business aspect of the area, but the impetus given by the Area Group has laid a good foundation for further developments.

The observation car – run as the last vehicle on the 10.15 Inverness–Kyle train – has been especially popular with tourists, and on 28 September 1987 a couple from Newcastle-on-Tyne received a bottle of champagne and complementary 'RailRover' tickets when they were the 5000th (and 5001st) passengers on the car in the May–October 1987 season. In 1986 a former LMS Engineer's Inspection saloon replaced a vehicle leased from Steamtown, Carnforth, but public complaints about the rough riding of the old LMS saloon brought another replacement for the 1987 season. The Highlands & Islands Development Board shared with BR the costs of converting a DMU trailer for use as an observation car, and this appears to have been well received. Carryings in the car in 1987 were double those of 1986, contributing to an overall increase of 25 per cent in revenue on the line between 1986 and 1987. This followed a 14 per cent increase between 1985 and 1986.

Additional services have been introduced gradually to keep up with increased demand. By 1987 the extra traffic warranted a fourth return Inverness–Kyle train daily except Fridays and Saturdays. This train in 1987 was normally made up of Mk2 airbraked stock, said to be the first regular working of such stock on the line.

Tourist traffic is the dominant source of the line's revenue, a point clearly made in The Highland Rail Study, carried out by consultants for BR and the Highlands & Islands Development Board. The Study Report, published in 1982, estimated a total of 126,000 passenger journeys on the line in 1980, of which only 16,300 were made by local residents. About half of the tourists travelling said that they would not have journeyed into the area if there were no railway, underlining the railway's contribution to the economy of the area.

As well as increasing revenue, the Business Group made good progress in reducing operating costs. By July 1984 all stations between Dingwall and Kyle were unstaffed. Friday, 13 July 1984, saw the official inauguration of Radio Electronic Token Block (RETB) signalling between Dingwall and Kyle, and with the installation of spring points, no signalmen or boxes were now required at intermediate crossing loops. Capital costs were calculated to be covered within two years due to operating cost savings, and the resulting improvement in the economic performance of the line must help in securing its continued operation, though at the cost of losing the personal service that was such a feature of its stations, as well as the local employment.

Considerable cost savings were also achieved by the Area Civil Engineer's introduction of changed methods of permanent way maintenance. Termed 'Controlled Patched Sleepering', it took the place of expensive track re-laying and ensures the future of the track itself into the twenty-first century.

Other signs of recent progress include the reinstatement of a siding on the Down side next to the platform line at Kyle of Lochalsh in early 1986. This is to accommodate the numerous special passenger trains working over the line during the summer season, including 'The Royal Scotsman', a prestige train with sleeping and dining cars which offers tourists, especially from overseas markets, a most comfortable scenic journey through Scotland. Also in 1986, electric heating replaced steam heating on trains operating on the line.

More recently, the refurbished Kyle of Lochalsh Station was opened on 17 June 1987 by Mr A. Russell, Convener of Highland Regional Council, reflecting the Council's financial assistance with the project and its close interest in railways in the Region.

The possibility of a freight resurgence appeared in 1987, with trial runs of timber from Kyle on wagons attached to passenger trains – a return to the mixed trains so characteristic of the line in earlier years. It was hoped that this would lead to a regular and sizeable traffic from the maturing forests on the west coast, but at the time of writing this has not materialised.

When assessing the prospects for a railway whose operating costs seem likely always to exceed its revenue by a considerable margin, it seems dangerous to assume that the future is assured. There are too many factors affecting its prospects, not the least of which is a Government which likes to see market forces operating as freely as possible in public transport and elsewhere. Yet the Inverness Area Business Group's approach showed the best answer to critics who point to poor operating ratios and profitability prospects, and no doubt there is further potential for the development of passenger and freight markets under their respective Sectors.

In 1987, a blow was dealt to the progress made in developing traffic and tackling costs by Area Managers in the North and North East of Scotland when it was announced that ScotRail was to administer several Areas, including Inverness, from

Perth, starting in 1988. This reduction in management responsibility 'at the sharp end' in the local market place is seen as a way of cost-saving, but it reduces the potential for identifying and developing local markets and affects the morale of staff in the 'outposts' of the former Areas. The announcement caused dismay among politicians and public as well as railwaymen. Doubtless it is preferable to line closures, but it is one more sign of the financial pressures under which ScotRail and BR as a whole are operating.

The railways of the Highlands, and the people who run them and travel on them, fortunately have a resilience built into them from birth, as John Thomas has shown in this book. The story of Duncraig Halt illustrates this well. It was listed for closure in the 1960s and subsequently omitted from the timetables. But the trains just kept on calling at the platform, and in 1976 Highland Regional Council suggested to BR that they should do the honourable thing, recognise reality and restore Duncraig to the timetable. To their great credit, BR agreed.

Nature also tested the resilience of the railway system on the morning of 7 February 1989, when the heavily swollen River Ness brought about the collapse of the railway bridge carrying the North line over the river. Many people were quick to point out that this event had been foretold by soothsayer Kenneth MacKenzie ('The Brahan Seer') in the 17th century but, undeterred by this event, ScotRail immediately organized connecting bus services between Inverness and Dingwall, there being fortunately sufficient stock including Class 37 locomotives on the marooned lines to the north. The day after the disaster, consulting engineers were appointed to design a replacement bridge, probably to be a two-span structure, the target date for opening being set for May 1990. The remains of the old bridge were 'delisted' allowing demolition to take place. Statements assuring rail users that there was full commitment to the re-establishment of the connection were also issued quickly in order to stem fears for the future of the Kyle and Wick/Thurso lines.

In the meantime, the observation car for the Kyle line, together with Class 156 Sprinter units intended for the summer

1989 services, could not be transferred from Inverness in the usual way, so these were transported by road in March and April to Muir of Ord where a temporary maintenance depot was established.

The summer 1989 services saw four daily return services from Dingwall to Kyle, three Sprinters and one locomotive hauled. The new road across the Black Isle made for comfortable bus connection times from Inverness, and traffic held up well, indeed much better than at the end of the steam era. So the 'Skye Line' remains very much in business, though specials cannot of course be resumed until the new Ness bridge is completed.

Some uncertainty, however, there will always be. The 1983 Serpell Report on Railway Finances resurrected the outmoded way of viewing railways purely in terms of internal costs and revenue, and for a time it looked as if Scotland might conceivably lose all of its lines north of Glasgow and Edinburgh. The threat was soon vanquished as the narrow evaluation methods used in the report were exposed for what they were. Any view of the value of lines like the Skye Line must take account of its socio-economic inputs into the area, and its heritage value as part of the tourist resource that the Highlands are. Narrow cost-revenue appraisal will not do any more, though, any reduction in the 'deficit' will be welcome. It is up to those of us who enjoy and appreciate railways like the Skye Line, as well as those charged with the responsibility of running them commercially, to ensure that they continue to run as working railways through to the twenty-first century and beyond, though any sudden drive to reduce the nation's rail system, perhaps under the impetus of privatisation, would again – if only temporarily – lead to debate about whether Inverness should be the end of the line.

Chronology

24 April 1864	First meeting of the promoters of the D & S Railway held in London
5 July 1865	The Dingwall & Skye Railway Act receives Royal Assent
29 May 1868	Dingwall & Skye (Deviation) Act receives Royal Assent
2 September 1868	First sod cut on Dingwall–Achanalt section
9 October 1868	First sod cut on Strathcarron section
19 August 1870	Railway opened Dingwall-Strome Ferry, 53 miles
9 November 1870	*Oscar* wrecked at Applecross
19 February 1871	Highland Railway takes over maintenance of line
31 July 1872	Strome Ferry engine shed burned down when engine cleaner upset can of oil
24 April 1877	Highland Railway (Steam Vessels) Act receives Royal Assent
1 September 1877	D & S Railway ceases steamboat operations
1 March 1878	Siding opened at Attadale
7 December 1878	Storm damages line between Attadale and Strome Ferry
10 June 1879	Accident at Achanalt. (Points wrongly set by stationmaster)
30 March 1880	*Carham* grounded at Raasay pier
17 April 1880	Highland Railway ceases steamboat operations

2 August 1880   Highland and Dingwall & Skye Railway
                    Companies (Amalgamation) Act receives
                    Royal Assent
1 September 1880   D & S Railway amalgamated with Highland
                    Railway
12 October 1881   Fish traffic agreement signed between High-
                    land, Caledonian and Callander & Oban
                    Railways
5 December 1881   High tide and gales cause severe damage to
                    line between Strathcarron and Strome Ferry
3 November 1882   7.50am Strome Ferry-Dingwall mixed train
                    derailed at Strathpeffer (Achterneed)
26 January 1884   Line blocked at several places following
                    severe snowstorm
3 June 1885   Strathpeffer branch opened from Fodderty
                    Junction
14 August 1890   Garve & Ullapool Railway Act receives
                    Royal Assent
16 October 1891   Strome Ferry station and 14 carriages and
                    vans destroyed by fire
14 October 1892   Accident at Achnashellach. Runaway train
29 June 1893   Highland Railway Act 1893 receives Royal
                    Assent. (Extension to Kyle of Lochalsh)
24 August 1893   Garve & Ullapool Railway (Abandonment)
                    Act receives Royal Assent
25 September
          1897   Runaway train near Raven Rock
2 November 1897   Railway opened to Kyle of Lochalsh
28 April 1908   Timber platform extension (40yd) author-
                    ised for Strathpeffer
13 June 1911   Highland Hotel, Strathpeffer opened
1 July 1914   Crossing loop at Luib opened
September 1916   'Loco smithy' established at Kyle of
                    Lochalsh
16 January 1919   Crossing loop at Loan (between Achnashel-
                    lach and Achnasheen) opened for Admiralty
                    purposes
10 May 1922   Sidings at Raven Rock authorised

May 1923	Raven Rock sidings re-authorised by LMS. Mid-Ross District Committee quarry
September 1937	Strome pier demolished
2 March 1946	Strathpeffer station closed to passengers
26 March 1951	Strathpeffer branch closed completely
March 1952	Raven Rock siding lifted
1 May 1954	Lochluichart station closed as part of the Conon Valley hydro-electric project. New station on deviation line opens 3 May 1954
26 March 1973	Ullapool-Stornoway sailing replaces Kyle-Stornoway
17 March 1975	Kyle-Portree mailboat service ends
Summer Season 1983	Sunday excursion trains Inverness–Kyle introduced successfully.
7 September 1983	Inverness Area Business Group formed to maximise revenue, minimise costs and improve services.
By Spring 1984	All stations on Kyle Line repainted in Highland Railway green and cream, with re-signing and new platform lighting.
13 July 1984	Radio Electronic Token Block Signalling inaugurated by Sir Peter Parker, Chairman of BR Board. Investment was £415,000. Stations between Dingwall and Kyle now unstaffed. Hydraulically sprung points installed and no signalmen required at intermediate crossing loops.
March 1986	Reinstatement of a siding at Kyle station to accommodate special passenger trains including 'The Royal Scotsman'. ETH replaces steam heating on the Kyle line.
Summer Season 1986	Ex-LMS Engineers' Inspection Saloon introduced as observation car, but rough riding arouses complaints.
Early 1987	Several trial consignments of timber conveyed from Kyle.
March 1987	Kyle of Lochalsh Pier (formerly owned by

ScotRail) sold to Highland Regional Council.

Summer Season 1987	Converted DMU coach (partly financed by HIDB) used as observation car and proves popular.
17 June 1987	Refurbished Kyle Station opened by A. Russell, Convener of Highland Regional Council.
January 1988.	Inverness Area Manager function discontinued, to be relocated in Perth.
7 February 1989	Ness Bridge at Inverness collapses in flood and lines to the north worked as self-contained unit. Small servicing depot created at Muir of Ord and bus connections provided to Dingwall. Decision rapidly taken to rebuild bridges.
Summer Season 1989	Sprinters introduced as planned.

Acknowledgements

Most of the source material on which this book is based is housed in the Scottish Record Office. I am indebted to the Keeper of the Records of Scotland and his staff for their excellent service. Documents created by the railway companies are reproduced with the approval of the Keeper of the Records of Scotland. I am also glad to acknowledge assistance given by Messrs George Barbour, A.G. Dunbar, P.J. Lane, J.F. McEwan, and the late Jack Templeton.

John Thomas

I am grateful to Messrs Bill Wood (formerly ScotRail Area Manager, Inverness) and Tom Haggarty (Train crew supervisor, Inverness) for their efforts in providing information, and privileged trips 'at the front end'.

Messrs Archie Roberts (Public transport officer) and David Summers (Public transport assistant) of Highland Regional Council have been most helpful in checking my efforts: any remaining errors are solely my responsibility.

I am also pleased to thank Dr W. A. Sharman and Alan Mitchell for their fine photographs of recent scenes on the line.

J. H. Farrington

Bibliography

Parliamentary Papers
Dingwall & Skye Railway Act 1865
Dingwall & Skye Railway (Deviation) Act 1868
Highland Railway (Steam Vessels) Act 1877
Highland and Dingwall & Skye Railway Companies Amalgamation Act 1880
Garve & Ullapool Railway Act 1890
Garve & Ullapool Railway (Abandonment) Act 1893
Highland Railway Act 1893 (Lochalsh Extension)
Parliamentary Debates (Selected)
Command Paper C 6946 (Report and correspondence concerning accident at Achnashellach 14 November 1892)
Report of the Rural Transport (Scotland) Committee 1918

Dingwall & Skye Railway records
Minute books 1864–80
Directors' reports to the shareholders and accounts 1869–80

Highland Railway records
Minutes books 1864–1922
Directors' reports to the shareholders 1864–1922
Agreement between the Highland Railway and David MacBrayne re West Coast shipping services 1880
Locomotive department notice book
Advertisement books 1904–22
Press cutting books (Various dates)
Working and public timetables

London Midland & Scottish Railway records
Minute books of Scottish Local Committee 1923–44
Deed of Agreement between LMS and MacBrayne's Trust Ltd
   re Kyle-Kyleakin ferry rights
Specification for turntable ferryboat *Kyleakin* 1930
Curves and lines over which engines may travel
Excursions and Advertising 1931–34
Working and public timetables

Miscellaneous
Minute books of the Great North of Scotland Railway 1891–93
Northern Chronicle
Glasgow Herald
Railway Times
Reminiscences of My Life in the Highlands Vol 2 Joseph Mitchell

Later Publications
Highland Rail Study. Prepared by Transmark/TRRU and sponsored by the Highlands & Islands Development Board and BR, 1982.

Railway Finances. Report of a committee chaired by Sir David Serpell, HMSO. 1983.

Index